GOGGLEBOOK

THE WIT & WISDOM OF GOGGLEBOX

Andrew Collins is an award-winning scriptwriter, journalist, author, critic and broadcaster whose hit BBC1 sitcom *Not Going Out* (co-written with star Lee Mack) won the Rose d'Or for Best Sitcom. He wrote two series of *Mr Blue Sky* for BBC Radio 4, was a regular scriptwriter on *EastEnders* and was a script consultant on *The Inbetweeners 2*. He has written three volumes of autobiography, including the bestselling *Where Did It All Go Right?*, and musician Billy Bragg's official biography. A presenter on BBC 6 Music for over ten years, he is currently the Film Editor of *Radio Times*, a TV critic for the *Guardian* and presents *Saturday Night at the Movies* on Classic FM.

First published 2015 by Boxtree
an imprint of Pan Macmillan
20 New Wharf Road, London N1 9RR
Associated companies throughout the world
www.panmacmillan.com

ISBN 978-1-5098-0930-1 HB
ISBN 978-1-5098-1292-9 TPB

Programme and format © Studio Lambert
Interviews © Pan Macmillan
Illustrations © Quinton Winter
Photography © Jude Edginton
Additional Photography © Shutterstock
Dutourdumonde Photography
Featureflash
Debby Wong
Shaun Jeffers
Danor Aharon
Landmarkmedia
David Muscroft
Design © Unreal Ltd 2015

1 3 5 7 9 8 6 4 2

A CIP catalogue record for this book is available from the British Library.

Printed and bound by Estella

Visit **www.panmacmillan.com** to read more about all our books
and to buy them. You will also find features, author interviews and
news of any author events, and you can sign up for e-newsletters
so that you're always first to hear about our new releases.

GOGGLEBOOK

THE WIT & WISDOM OF GOGGLEBOX

Andrew Collins

Illustrations by Quinton Winter

BOXTREE

OI! DORIS

GOGGLEBOX SAY THEY WANNA FILM US READING THIS BOOK ABOUT US BEING FILMED WATCHING THE TELLY!

WELL BASIC. BET YA THEY STICK A CARTOON OF US IN THE FRONT OF THE BOOK ABOUT BEING ASKED TO BE FILMED READING THE BOOK ABOUT BEING FILMED WHILE WATCHING TELLY

WHO DO YOU THINK YOU ARE?

MYSTIC BLEEDIN' MEG?

MORE POINTLESS COBBLERS FOR THE DOWNSTAIRS LAV

NOW FOR SOMETHING MORE STIMULATING...

POLDARK

Foreword
The Gogglebox Grand Tour

I believe in *Gogglebox*. I maintain that it is a force for good in an often cruel world and its continued, growing popularity gives lie to any notion that it's just another reality-TV format. It might actually be the only true reality-TV format: unforced, natural and disarmingly honest. I'm a fan. Which is why I jumped at the unique opportunity of attempting the Grand Tour of *Gogglebox*: what turned out to be a 1,943-mile round trip to all of the current households. I caught a lot of connecting trains, tested a lot of local cab companies and ate a lot of biscuits.

Armed only with a Dictaphone, a camera and DVDs of specially chosen historic TV moments to watch with each household, I started in London, completed two major return excursions north, then mopped up the destinations that didn't require an overnight stay as awaydays. It felt like a really badly planned stay-cation, or a long-winded religious pilgrimage, and not once did I approach the next *Gogglebox* address without hearing that Kodaline song in my head about being in a perfect world. The one assurance I was given before setting off was that the collective *Gogglebox* family are exactly the same in real life as they come across on television. This turned out to be 100 per cent true. No illusions were shattered. No magic was destroyed. A modest degree of furniture rearrangement occurs in one or two of the houses, but that's pretty much it for the screen coming down on the Wizard of Oz.

Though the Goggleboxers never meet each other, in order to maintain the purity of the show (the same reason they are not all over the media), they are united in one aspect: all ardently keen to tell me how much they love the camera crews who invade their homes for hours on end during each series, and become part of the family. This feeling is reciprocated.

It has been a long, strange trip. Over four weeks, I met thirty-five Goggleboxers, six cats and seven dogs, plus three family members, one dog and one cat who aren't seen on TV, and one builder, John, who was working on Giles and Mary's downstairs loo. While emotionally demanding – you are, after all, in a complete stranger's front room hoping to make a good impression and yet you feel like you've been there before – it was always rewarding and endlessly entertaining. Sandra in south-west London said, 'Me and Sandy are good people.' They all are.

The result of my travels, which you now hold in your hands, is a collection of all of my favourite moments from the TV show so far, plus a wealth of brand-new, exclusive, unbroadcast material from the cast, as I fulfilled every *Gogglebox* fan's dream by sitting amongst them on their sofas and watching TV with them. I even got to watch classic TV moments from the past and travel back through time. It was a privilege and a constant, cross-country hoot. In a perfect world, I hope it feels like you were there with us, too.

Andrew Collins, 2015

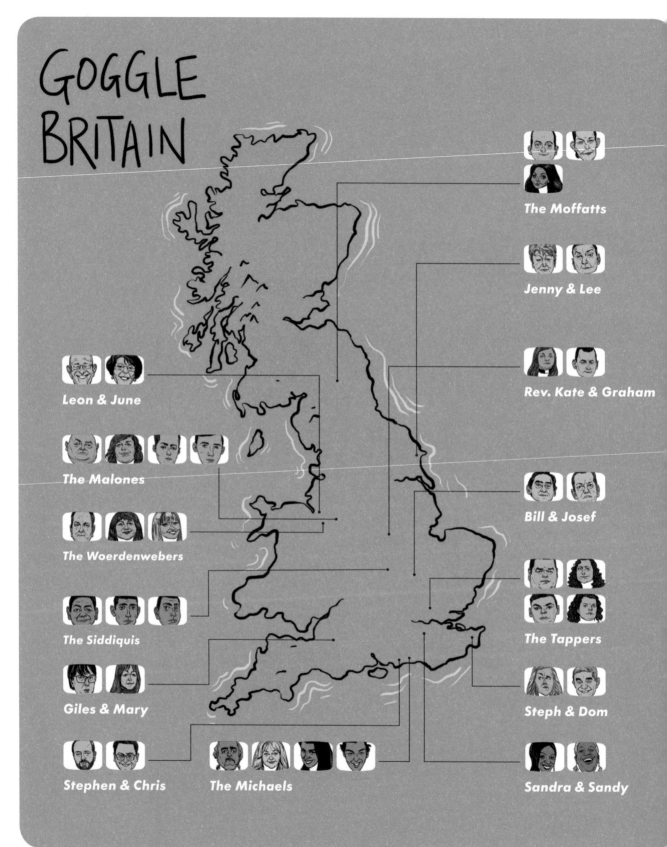

GOGGLE BRITAIN

The Moffatts

Jenny & Lee

Rev. Kate & Graham

Leon & June

The Malones

Bill & Josef

The Woerdenwebers

The Siddiquis

The Tappers

Giles & Mary

Steph & Dom

Stephen & Chris

The Michaels

Sandra & Sandy

GOGGLEBOX TV

Featuring
THE LETTER 'A'

Including
ALAN CARR: CHATTY MAN
ANTIQUES ROADSHOW
ANT & DEC'S SATURDAY NIGHT TAKEAWAY

Plus
THE APPRENTICE

EXCLUSIVE! Watching Alan Carr: Chatty Man with Sandy & Sandra!

Watching

ALAN CARR: CHATTY MAN

with SANDY AND SANDRA

Laughter is never far away at Sandra's home in south-west London. She and Sandy – friends since childhood – are protected from the world's ills by a force field of positivity, released in great guffaws. In their overwhelming company, you begin to see them as a pair of superheroes, waiting for the nod to save the planet.

Both women's hands are galvanized with hardware: rings, bracelets, charms and bejewelled watches. They are decoratively armed for battle. Where other folk have fruit in a fruit bowl, Sandra's is overflowing with jewellery. The first-floor flat was the only *Gogglebox* address I genuinely feared I wouldn't get into. Following instructions about numbers, gates, stairs and doorbells to the letter, I found myself

> 66
>
> Sandy:
>
> ***Babes! I'm in Armani! This tracksuit cost £200!***
>
> 99

marooned outside an unmarked door. I checked with a neighbour and she said, 'I heard them earlier.' I think I'd expected to hear them from the street outside. Finally, Sandra's face appeared at a window above me and they generously absorbed me into their world.

While Sandra, 53, fusses, insisting on getting changed for a snapshot for my album ('I got wigs here. I got a purple one, babes. I got this one for a family photo shoot. I'm just gonna go natural today. You get me?'), Sandy, 49, waits, confident in her attire: 'Babes, I'm in Armani! This tracksuit cost £200! The American top rappers have got this one Jay-Z and all them, babes. And guess what I got here? *Games of Thrones!*' She shows me a metal *Game of Thrones* Hand of the King brooch. In the show, it denotes the most powerful appointed position in the Seven Kingdoms, second only to the king. This seems apt, as the ever-affirmative Sandy happily defers to the woman known in their native Brixton as 'Queen B', who re-emerges wearing a diaphanous, psychedelic, radioactively orange top ('I paid £16 for this, from My Girl next to the pub'). Her hair is nipped with multicoloured bands into peroxided buds, so that the top of her head resembles the early result of a Play-Doh barber's shop figure. She carries it off. Sandy's hairdo is an explosion. I notice Sandra keeps repeating the mantra, 'Learn to breathe, learn to breathe,' and assume it's a self-help thing, but it's actually because the orange top is 'an inch tight'. She's trying to lose weight: 'I've got a salad today!'

Alan Carr: Chatty Man

FRIDAY, 10PM

C4 Northampton's favourite son is now into his fourteenth series of the sticky-drink-fuelled chat show. Among his guests tonight are *The Last Leg* trio, the stars of cop show *No Offence* and Noel Gallagher. Sandy and Sandra appeared on Alan's Christmas special in 2014, so feel a kinship.

Sandy: Look how many lampshades he's got in the studio, man.

A horse race plays silently on the flatscreen with the 'No regret in Jesus' sticker, and our time together gallops past in a whirl of boasts, banter, bonhomie, big-ups and the Brixton equivalent of blarney. There's no time to breathe. Or even to appreciate fully Sandra's 'shrine': a dresser covered in cards ('Love you, Grandma'), photos, cuttings, invites, souvenirs, toys, trinkets, a Bible and a sparkly cross. I feel underdressed just standing near it.

Sandy and Sandra magnanimously allow me to ease in between them as we gear up to watch Alan Carr: Chatty Man, with the sound of costume jewellery tapping on mugs.

Sandy: My boy. Our friend. He makes me laugh.

Sandra: I love his trousers. He's got big feet, you know!

Sandy: His feet *are* big.

Sandra: Alan's lost a bit of weight. He ain't got a belly too much. Noel Gallagher – he was on *Gogglebox* with Kate Moss and Naomi.

Sandy: I said to her, 'Stay away, yeah?'

Sandra: *The Last Leg*? I watched their election thing the other day. That's how I know them. What's the gossip, Alan?

Sandy: Look how many lampshades he's got in the studio, man.

Sandra: I'm surprised he's allowed to say certain things he says.

Sandy: I think they must check the script before.

Alan makes a joke about placing a bet on the royal baby's name being 'Croissant', which is funny in the context of the rather elaborate set-up. Sandy and Sandra love it.

Sandra: Croissant. Charlotte. You get me?

Another topical gag about the hypnotist dog on Britain's Got Talent; another slam-dunk in the room.

Sandra: He has lost weight because usually his jacket's tight and it's very loose now.

The Last Leg trio come on, en masse: Adam Hills, Alex Brooker and Josh Widdicombe; and the first comment is that Chatty Man lacks a ramp.

Sandy: I like them. They're funny. Take those three off that programme with the cars, and put these three on.

Sandra: He's still on the booze, though. He's got a bottle of rum shaped like a pistol. I want one of those!

Brooker tells a tale of his new realistic prosthetic leg and the downside of sunbathing in it.

Sandra: Ain't he got no legs either?

Sandy: He has got legs. I think he has. It's just his hands and arms.

Sandra: *Chatty Man*'s got some dodgy drinks.

Sandy: That one he brought out back in the day (for Courtney Love)…that woman got drunk.

Sandra: She got tipsy, she was all over the place.

Sandy: It makes you more relaxed. (pointing out Adam Hills) He's got one foot.

Sandra: Really? They're all Paralympics?

Except Widdicombe.

Sandy: I love that. They need to do more things like that. Remember before? You could not be on there with one leg or one arm, nothing like that.

Sandy:

Chatty Man's got some dodgy drinks.

Sandra: (eureka moment) That's why it's called *The Last Leg*!

Sandy: Hey, I saw a newsreader with a burkha on! You could see her eyes and her face. On normal television, reading the news! I've never seen that before. That is diversity – it's coming in. They've got that Indian guy that does that show. He actually chats.

Sandra: He's holding that bottle tight – he's not letting it go.

Sandy: When we met Alan Carr, he's just the same.

Sandra: I don't get to watch him now cos there's other programmes on. *Big Brother*'s on when he comes on at 10pm. He ain't had no one hot on the show lately.

A bottle of something blue is passed round. Brooker knocks his back in one and regrets it.

Sandy: I've got that! I've got that! I've got that! That blue one! I've got that! It's a liqueur.

Sandra: I don't know how they can do it.

Sandy: He backed it. He's sweating, look! Oh my God! 'It's burning in my chest, Alan!'

How was your experience with Alan?

Sandra: It was lovely. I met whatshisname, *Celebrity Juice*…Keith Lemon!

Sandy: And that woman whose boyfriend is a footballer, Abbey Clancy.

> ❝
>
> Sandra:
>
> **We've had some good times with Gogglebox, man. The best times of my life.**
>
> ❞

SANDRA'S TV ROUTINE

6am *Good Morning Britain*, ITV

9.15am *The Wright Stuff*, Channel 5
'I also do a bit of Jeremy Kyle because I like to hear a bit of deep gossip.'

11.30am *The Real Housewives of Atlanta*, ITV2
'Then the news comes on.'

2pm *Judge Rinder*, ITV
'I know him, he's my mate.'

3–6pm
'In the afternoon, I might do a little movie.'

6pm *ITV News*

7pm *Emmerdale*, ITV
'My phone is locked off!'

7.30pm *Coronation Street*

8pm *EastEnders*

9pm *Big Brother*
'If it's on.'

Sandra: And Corden. He's gone to America now.

Sandy: The comedian with the curly hair, he was there as well. Quite stocky.

Sandra: We've had some good times with *Gogglebox*, man. The best times of my life. I like *Chatty Man* when they've got good guests on. I don't know who these guests are.

I hate to leave this certified safe place, but my jaw is sore from hilarity. 'We're not toffee-nosed yet,' Sandra declares, polishing off the cupcake I brought as a gift. 'I'm always at the bus stop, babes. Me and Sandy are good people. Paparazzi are not outside in our bins or across the road peeping, because I'll tell you something, any time I see them, I got a pee bucket. No, I got a bucket of Fairy Liquid water, waiting.'

Laughter follows me back into the outside world – but, to my relief, no water.

Antiques Roadshow

SUNDAY, 8PM

BBC1 The BBC's flagship antique/junk appraisal show has been travelling the country, encouraging us to rummage through our attics and see if we have anything worth a fortune, since 1977. For many of us it has come to define Sunday-evening telly.

 Sandy: Posh car-boot sale!

 Dom: Sunday evening isn't Sunday evening without the *Antiques Roadshow*.

 Stephen: What this programme does is that after a heavy weekend, you can sit in front of the box, cross-eyed and bored to death, and not have to think about anything, apart from you have to get up for work tomorrow.

 Giles: I fantasise about how much money I might make from selling the corner cupboard.

 Alex Michael: Is this the one with the red and the blue teams?

 Louis Michael: That's *Bargain Hunt*.

 Rev. Kate: How much? Yeah, alright, how much? Yeah, Russian artist, la la la, *how much*?

 Stephen: Stop prattling on about it. How much?

 Sandra: How much?!

 June: I wonder …

 Leon: Would you not talk when they're giving the value?

 Chris: Most of them are like, 'No, I'd never sell it.'

 Stephen: The thing is, at that age, there's no point in keeping it. I might as well flog it and have a jolly-up.

 Baasit Siddiqui: The rain never falls on *Antiques Roadshow*, does it? They must pick the one sunny day in England each year and just film all the episodes then.

Baasit Siddiqui:

I just get bitter that between all of us we don't have one antique.

Sid Siddiqui:

Apart from me.

Baasit Siddiqui:

But you're priceless.

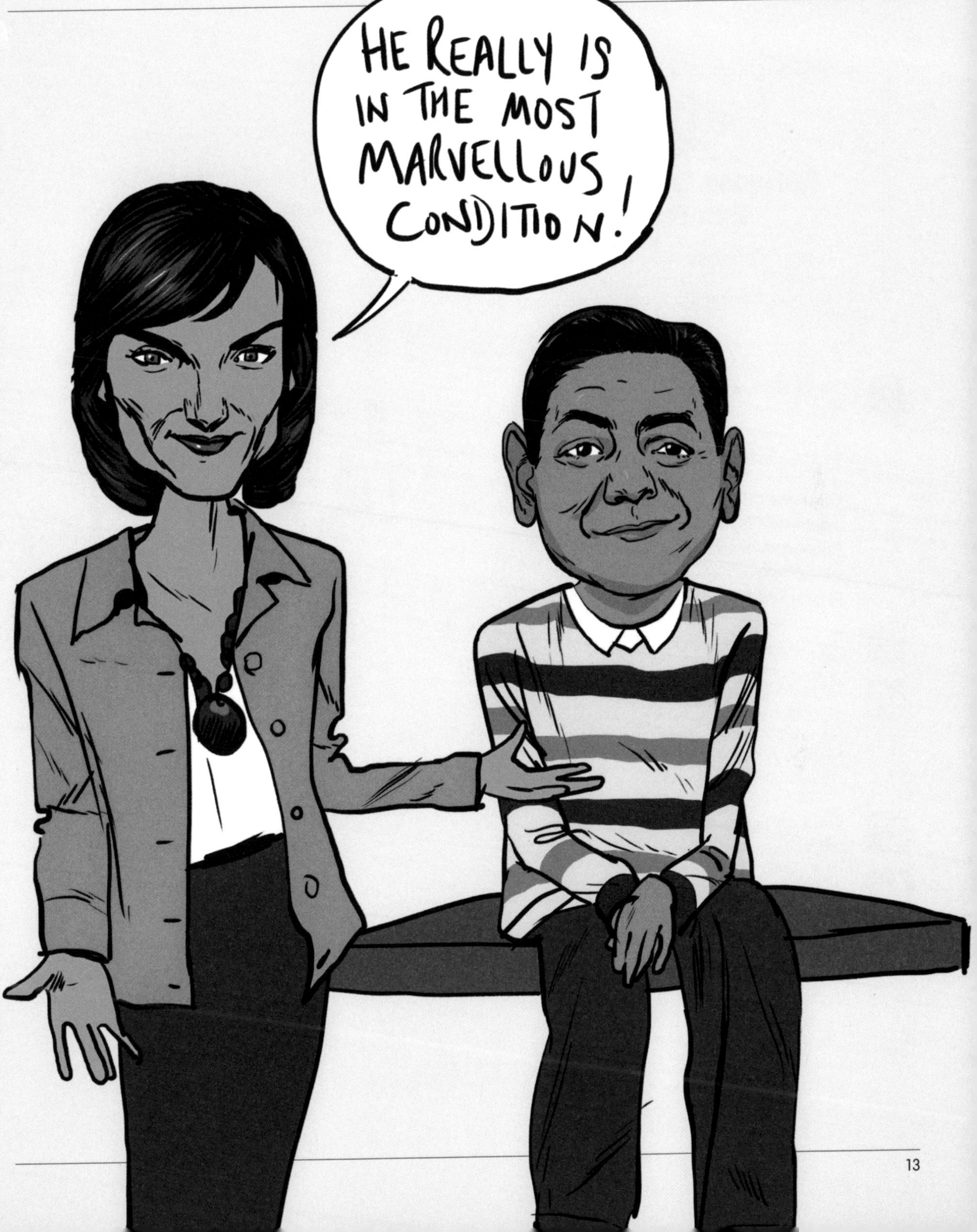
HE REALLY IS IN THE MOST MARVELLOUS CONDITION!

Antiques Roadshow Fun Fact

Apparently the Queen herself is a fan.

Umar Siddiqui: I'm always a little bit on edge, though. Like someone's gonna get murdered. It's like a country house, a garden party. It's basically *Midsomer Murders*.

Over the years, the show has been presented by Bruce Parker, Angela Rippon, Arthur Negus, Hugh Scully and Michael Aspel. It is currently presented by Fiona Bruce.

Sandra: Is that Sarah Beeny?

Baasit Siddiqui: Fiona Bruce just does the news and this. I reckon she wants to show the world she has legs and a bottom half. She looks younger every time I see her. She's like Benjamin Button.

Sid Siddiqui: She's a typical example of how you should keep an antique.

June: I think she's brilliant at this.

Leon: Not a big enough bust.

ANTIQUES ROADSHOW TV BINGO

A person clearly disappointed with how little their antique is worth but claiming, 'Oh, we'd never part with it!'

A repair that has substantially lowered the value

Red trousers!

An antique that has been used in a way other than it was first intended – i.e. to keep biros in

A member of the public in a straw hat who appears in the background more than three times

A letter of provenance

A sad toy that's still pristine in its box and has never been played with by a child

Arundel Castle

A chipped Toby jug

Watching
ANTIQUES ROADSHOW
with JENNY AND LEE

 Retired publican Jenny, 60, and retired bingo manager Lee, 47, give off the sunny disposition of being permanently on holiday. It's a prematurely hot May day when I meet them, which helps.

When they're not filming in Jenny and her husband Ray's static caravan – note: 'caravan' is properly pronounced with the emphasis on 'van' for the full Yorkshire effect – Jenny and Lee are in Cyprus, where both now have holiday homes. The 40-acre leisure park where Jenny and Ray have had the van for two years with its bar, restaurant,

> **66**
>
> Jenny:
>
> *You had more chandeliers than Buckingham Palace.*
>
> **99**

spa, sauna, pool and steam room will continue to act as her and Lee's semi-iconic *Gogglebox* address. On the day of my visit, Ray, busy rustling up delicious bacon and fried-mushroom sandwiches in the correct soft white sliced bread, is rhapsodizing about last night's cracking multiple tribute-act bill, featuring Michael Bublé and Amy Winehouse. Just being here is like a break from your own everyday life. We sit down to watch *Antiques Roadshow*. The 38-year-old bric-a-brac valuation flagship parks up at Lowther Castle in Cumbria. Jenny gets out her famous 'tin plate', which she passionately believes is 'worth something'.

Jenny: I've got this tin plate …

Lee: Not you and that bastard tin plate again.

Jenny: The string on the back's real old. I'm gonna take it somewhere.

Lee: I wish you would so we could watch *Antiques Roadshow* without you going on about your bloody tin plate.

The handling of said item reveals it to the untrained eye to be at least a couple of years old. Lee sighs deeply while Jenny's husband, Ray, plugs the DVD player in. Jenny is already humming along to the theme.

Jenny: Arthur Negus used to do it, you know.

Another deep sigh of disengagement from Lee.

Lee: It just shows you how much tat people have in their house.

Jenny: You haven't!

Lee: I haven't got a house!

Jenny: Yeah, but when you had a house it were like Liberace's.

Lee: Thanks a lot.

Jenny: You had more chandeliers than Buckingham Palace. Oh, Fiona Bruce has got that frock on again.

Lee: I don't know who does her wardrobe lately. She needs Gok Wan. They never used to have this little history lesson at the beginning of *Antiques Roadshow* before.

Lee:

Not you and that bastard tin plate again.

A man in the castle grounds offers up a ring he found under a park bench when he was eight years old, which he has kept ever since.

Jenny: Really?

Lee: Hand it in, you thieving little bastard.

Our expert explains that its value 'rests on the stone'. If it is indeed a Burmese ruby, then the man's casual find would be worth 'several hundreds of thousands of pounds'.

Jenny: What?!

There's one slight problem: it's not.

Jenny: (with glee) It's paste. I bet he's gutted! I bet he's fuming.

It's still theoretically worth 'four to five hundred'.

Jenny: Oh, that's nice. He'll have to get it to the pawn shop. That's what I like about this programme, when they think it's really worth a lot of money … (distracted by a child's toy) Ooh, it's a little car!

Lee: I'd guess about two grand.

Jenny: I'm going to say... £1,700.

The expert points out that the child's car was made 'by appointment to His Majesty'.

Jenny: Ooh, five grand. If you buy a pork pie that's appointment to the Queen it's double the price.

Lee is about to gainsay, but hears the expert mention 'anybody in the Cockermouth area' and starts giggling.

Lee: You just wouldn't live there, would you?

Jenny changes her mind at the last minute.

Jenny: A thousand pound.

The toy car is valued at 'between £1,500 and £2,000'.

Jenny: I got it right.

Lee: You changed it! Sorry, but you went to £5,000, then £1,000.

Jenny: (distracted again) Ooh, Harrogate!

A hand-illustrated book dated 1917 is offered up; it's bound in rat skin.

Jenny: Eurgh. They'll have bashed it with a rolling pin and rolled it out. Or just used a few rats.

Lee: It's been stretched.

It's valued at £5,000.

Lee: For a piece of f**king rat skin.

Jenny: They should have left the tail on for a bookmark!

Some vases from Lowther Castle itself are revealed to be worth 'about £20'.

Lee: I bet the boxes she brought 'em in cost more.

Some vintage Action Man dolls are shown.

Jenny: Lee used to dress his Action Man up in little frocks.

A medal is valued at 'at least £5,000'.

Jenny: Really? Again! Ooh, I keep saying 'really'. It's all I ever say.

When it's time for me to leave, I touch Jenny's plate once for luck, then step out into the early-evening sunshine. In my mildly euphoric state, Hull has never looked so beautiful. Cab back to the city centre: £22. An afternoon with Jenny and Lee: priceless.

—— 66 ——

Jenny:

Lee used to dress his Action Man up in little frocks.

—— 99 ——

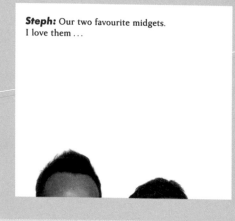

Steph: Our two favourite midgets. I love them . . .

Ant & Dec's Saturday Night Takeaway

SATURDAY, 7PM

ITV Beloved Geordie tag-presenters Anthony McPartlin and Declan Donnelly were child actors on *Byker Grove*, chart stars as PJ & Duncan ('Psyche!') and now Mr and Mr Saturday Night TV with their own ragbag format.

 Rev. Kate: It's just brilliant Saturday-night telly.

 Viv Woerdenweber: I don't know where they get their energy from. They're always bouncing around.

 Steph: Our two favourite midgets. I love them. My favourite's Dec.

 Dom: That's only cos he gave you the eye when he passed you on the M3.

 Josh Tapper: It's the best programme.

 Dom: Watching them is a bit like watching Torvill and Dean: you sort of get the impression they've had sex together; they know each other inside out.

 June: It's like the old shows, isn't it?

 Leon: It's rubbish, absolute rubbish. I would put them down. They're absolutely hopeless. The only one I like is Amanda Holden because she's attractive and she's got a good figure.

 Sandra: Which one's Ant and which one's Dec? I have never known the difference.

 Baasit Siddiqui: To hate Ant and Dec is to hate life.

Ant & Dec Fun Fact

Ant & Dec have lived near each other since they were 14, first as flat mates, then neighbours, and now on the same road.

> Dom:
>
> **Watching them is a bit like watching Torvill and Dean.**

HOW TO TELL ANT & DEC APART

An illustrated guide

2 inches

Ant is 2 inches taller.

Ant also has a larger forehead than Dec.

Ant always stands on the left.

Dec always stands on the right.

The Apprentice

WEDNESDAY, 9PM

BBC1 Gladiatorial recruitment competition in which the least sweet Sugar ever fires people he doesn't even employ yet.

Bill: I'm sure I'd never employ anyone who used the phrase 'thinking outside the box'.

 Rev. Kate: I love this show.

 June: He's quite handsome in a rugged sort of way.

 Bill: I'd never employ anyone who used the phrase 'thinking outside the box'.

 Stephen: I'm surprised he still does it. I'm surprised he's not bored. But I suppose it's easy money for him to sit there and say, 'You're fired'.

YOU'RE FIRED!

WELL 'TECHNICALLY' I HAVEN'T ACTUALLY HIRED YOU YET. SO I SUPPOSE IT WOULD BE MORE CORRECT TO SAY YOU'RE NOT HIRED.

21

Alan Sugar Fun Fact

Lord Sugar is a qualified pilot with over thirty years' experience. In 2010 he bought a private jet and registered it as G-SUGA.

Dom: I'm sure half of them are employed for their stupidity.

Chris: I really like this because all of the idiots on here think they're something special. And every week they're proved they're actually a bunch of divs.

Andrew Michael: They're always ghastly, arrogant, aggressive, overconfident.

Leon: They're crawling to him. I don't like the programme at all.

Steph: I get irritated because they're very petty, juvenile arguments and I would never sit at a board table and listen to that.

Dom: I'd just tell them to shut up.

Scarlett Moffatt: Ah, she's made a right tit of herself.

June: Remember when you had a go at your dad's business?

Leon: I didn't like it.

June: You let the customers walk away, didn't even engage them in conversation.

Leon: I'm an entertainer.

THE APPRENTICE TV BINGO

A promise to give 110 per cent	Someone taking credit for someone else's work in the boardroom	An annoying team name like 'Alpha', 'Stealth' or 'Synergy'
Two candidates on the same team talking over each other on the phone	A dodgy CV being exposed in the interviews round	Fist pump/high five/ group hug
Lord Sugar using a Cockney phrase you've never even heard on *EastEnders*	A male candidate with intricate facial hair	A female candidate claiming to have 'balls'

GOGGLEBOX TV

Featuring
THE LETTER 'B'

Including
BARACK OBAMA
BASIC INSTINCT
BEAR GRYLLS
BERLIN WALL

Plus
BISCUITS
BRIAN COX
BRITAIN'S GOT TALENT

and
BRITNEY SPEARS

EXCLUSIVE! Watching Britain's Got Talent with the Tappers!

★ THE GOGGLEBOX ★

MAGICAL HISTORY TOUR

Through the power of TV, we take you back to 2008

Barack Obama (the election of)

The first black president of the United States, the first to be born in Hawaii, and the first with Kenyan ancestry, elected with a popular majority of 51.1 per cent in November 2008, at which point the world went nuts with hope. We watch a news report on the way that the election result was reported around the world.

Lee: Forty-fourth president? I didn't know there'd been that bastard many.

 Jenny: He has been a good president, though.

 Lee: Has he? He's doing adverts now.

 Jenny: Yeah, stupid ones. But he's got a lovely smile, hasn't he?

 Mark Moffatt: I always thought Americans are that crazy, he'd be assassinated.

 Scarlett Moffatt: That must have been mental for them, because only a couple of decades before, black people had to sit at the back of buses and everything. And all of a sudden: black president. It's crazy. I bet some of them older people never thought they'd see the day. And we'll see the first woman president soon.

 Mark Moffatt: They love their politics much more than us, don't they?

 Scarlett Moffatt: I think they look at him as a leader, but none of us really look at David Cameron as a leader. We just think of him as a prime minister.

 Betty Moffatt: At the time they must have thought he was absolutely gonna change the world.

 Rev. Kate: I once heard someone explaining the difference between Republicans and Democrats. They said Republicans are a bit like our Tory party, and the Democrats are a bit like our Tory party. It's like the choice between Coke and Pepsi.

 Tom Malone: He's a cool dude, isn't he?

 Tom Malone Jnr: He's got big ears.

 Shaun Malone: I feel they characterized him due to the colour of his skin. As they were taking a step forward, they were taking a step backward.

"

Tom Malone:

He's a cool dude, isn't he?

"

 Jonathan Tapper: People voted for him because he was the first black president. It's like showbiz. It's like watching a film. And he had no competition.

 Josh Tapper: He blew his opportunity to be a really historical president. He hasn't done a great job.

 June: That really was history being made.

 Leon: It wasn't just black people celebrating. It was wonderful. Hillary Clinton will walk it, you watch.

 Stephen: I'm glad he got in. I want Hillary to get in next.

 Chris: We might end up with a black prime minister here.

 Stephen: That Chuka Umunna's going to be a big knob someday. That's why Labour got in down here in Hove: Peter Kyle's good-looking.

 Baasit Siddiqui: Tupac was wrong. He said, 'We ain't ready to see a black president.'

 Umar Siddiqui: This was the most popular Obama's ever been.

 Baasit Siddiqui: He was always going to under-deliver, wasn't he?

 Ralf Woerdenweber: People were getting nuts, crying, dancing, partying. On the other hand, it is a 24/7 job and you grow older really quickly. Five years is like fifteen years.

Stephen: This is the beaver bit. Come on. Show us your minge.

Basic Instinct

18 Channel 5-preceding erotic thriller, directed by Paul Verhoeven and starring Michael Douglas and Sharon Stone, primarily famous for an iconic scene in which Stone's vamp, Catherine Tramell, uncrosses her legs to reveal she's forgotten her knicks.

Leon: Have you seen this?

June: No.

Leon: Oooooh. It'll turn you on, June.

June: I'm sure it will.

Jenny: Is it a Disney film?

Lee: (stares at Jenny)

Graham: I went to see this at the cinema with my sister and brother-in-law.

Rev. Kate: You went to see this with your sister?!

Graham: They didn't know what it was. They nearly walked out, I think.

Rev. Kate: (long pause) You went to see it with your sister.

When it was time for THAT scene with Sharon Stone in the chair …

Umar Siddiqui: Dad, you probably don't want to watch this.

Sid Siddiqui: I've seen it.

Umar Siddiqui: Not with your sons.

 June: Are we leading up to some sort of important event?

 Leon: Just wait.

 Stephen: This is the beaver bit. Come on. Show us your minge.

The scene happens.

 Scarlett Moffatt: You actually see her foof. I think I've had a mini sick in my mouth.

 Sandra: If I was young, I'd do the same. But with my bad knee…

 Leon: It's just as shocking now as it was then.

 June: You think?

 Leon: I do – showing your pokie to the world.

 Scarlett Moffatt: If you were flashing your vulva at a policeman, they'd say, 'Come on, that's not appropriate.' And they'd go and get her some pants from the lost-and-found box. They wouldn't be letting her sit on that seat. It's unhygienic.

 Baasit Siddiqui: That was the first time a lady garden got shown on TV.

 Umar Siddiqui: A lot of people did poorly on their GCSEs from this film.

 Stephen: If I ever get nicked, I'm gonna do that: 'What are you gonna do, harass me?'

 Chris: And then flash your fanny.

Baasit Siddiqui:

That was the first time a lady garden got shown on TV.

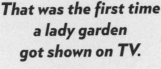

Bear Grylls

Bear Grylls is an overeducated former SAS reservist, adventurer, mountaineer, parachutist and all-round action figure, best known for survival skills and drinking his own wee.

Dom:

I used to think Bear Grylls was one of those grill things where the fat drips off the side.

June: Did you know Bear Grylls is very religious?

 Leon: I know his name's stupid.

 Ralf Woerdenweber: I would like to do something with Bear Grylls. I grew up in Germany in forests, so I would see if his knowledge is so big. I don't believe so. I really don't. I think he is in the hotel, everyone else does it for him and then gives him the information and he steps in and says it on camera, and then he pisses off in the hotel. I say: Bear Grylls and me, in a helicopter, over the water, he jumps with me into the water and then…no camera teams. No first aid. No health and safety. No one, but him and me, going from here to there in five days. I'll see how he will do.

 Viv Woerdenweber: Probably never see Ralf again.

 Eve Woerdenweber: Bye, Ralf.

 Ralf Woerdenweber: The producers of that show must think we are all stupid. I would never drink pee out of a bottle. It is raining on the leaves on the tree; the real, nice water drip down. If I would be there, I'd put a bottle under there and it's full in ten minutes. And I would drink that nice, fresh water. I wouldn't pee in a bottle. It's stupid.

Baasit Siddiqui:

I have a T-shirt that says 'What would Bear Grylls do?' on it.

Bear Grylls Fun Fact

In 2009, Bear Grylls was appointed Chief Scout, becoming the youngest man to hold that office since the position was created for Robert Baden-Powell in 1920.

★ THE GOGGLEBOX ★

MAGICAL HISTORY TOUR

Through the power of TV, we take you back to 1989

Berlin Wall (the fall of the)

Almost literal 'Iron Curtain' put up in Berlin in 1961 to mark the divide between the Communist East and the decadent West; and primarily to stem defection from the East and the flow of Levi's jeans from the West. Euphorically rushed by East Germans after the domino-effect fall of state communism in November 1989, it was dismantled using tiny implements. The Goggleboxers and I watch some famous news footage and they talk about their memories of this momentous event.

Graham: I was gutted about this, because I'd just been on a holiday round Germany with a friend and we wanted to go to East Germany, but it took us so long to arrange all the paperwork that when it came down to it, they wouldn't let us in. And two months later, they knocked the wall down.

 Rev. Kate: Oh, I think I'm about to cry. It's the power of the people. There's nothing I like better than a group of enthusiastic people who believe in something. With the exception of the Nuremberg Rallies, obviously.

 Lee: I remember this. I can't believe it were that long ago. I bet they never thought they'd see the day.

 Jenny: Isn't it lovely, though, the way it all went? I'm all goosey. I bet it was really emotional.

 Lee: People kept bits of this wall, didn't they?

 Scarlett Moffatt: Wasn't David Hasselhoff there?

 Betty Moffatt: He's massive in Germany for some reason. There's no accounting for taste, is there?

 Scarlett Moffatt: Why did they take it down then? You'd get shot if you went over the wall?

 Betty Moffatt: I went on a school trip to Germany when I was about fifteen and went to visit. (commenting on the action on the telly) You're not going to do anything with a hammer that size, are you? Better off using a spoon.

 Giles: We were aware of it, it was going on in the background.

 Mary: But we had a small child bawling her head off.

 Giles: Also, we hadn't really studied modern history at school. But once we saw that film, *The Lives of Others,* we understood why it was such a big thing. We didn't realize how bad it was behind the Iron Curtain.

 Mary: And we didn't have a television between 1987 and 1999. We had the black-and-white set for part of it.

 Shaun Malone: Didn't Hasselhoff take it down?

 Tom Malone: He did a gig, and all the people on that side of the wall pulled it down to get away from it.

 Julie Malone: Look at the haircuts! Kajagoogoo style!

 Josh Tapper: Did they overthrow the government or what?

 Jonathan Tapper: It was the end of communism, so they didn't need the wall.

 Josh Tapper: So it wasn't really illegal what they were doing?

 Nikki Tapper: I was sixteen. I remember watching it. But I didn't realize how big it was.

 Jonathan Tapper: All the Eastern bloc countries, apart from Russia, became part of the European Union.

 Leon: *Ich bin ein Berliner.*

———— 66 ————

Julie Malone:

Look at the haircuts! Kajagoogoo style!

———— 99 ————

June: Our friend's son was there. He got a first in German.

 Leon: They shouldn't have got in the war, should they, the Germans?

 Stephen: The only thing I remember about this was David Hasselhoff singing on the top of it.

 Chris: I was thirteen.

 Stephen: I was eighteen. I was going to raves by then – I didn't give a f**k.

 Andrew Michael: I love this. November '89. I'd just had a lovely little baby daughter, Katy, who was six months old; I'd just sold my hotel for squillions: it was happy days. But they were really genuinely happy. This was a fantastic episode in history. Breathtaking. I'd studied so much history and all the books I'd read said that the division of Europe was very stable, and enduring, and would carry on and on.

 Carolyne Michael: I thought, as soon as that wall comes down, they're gonna run out of plots for James Bond.

 Sandy: I didn't really do the Berlin Wall, no. I only watch *Schindler's List*, babes, that's as far as I go.

 Sandra: We're not war people.

———— 66 ————

Stephen:

The only thing I remember was David Hasselhoff singing on top of it.

———— 99 ————

 Ralf Woerdenweber: Oh my God! We were living in Cologne. People sitting in my mum's pub were crying. My mum was from the East, so she was crying. Two years after, in '91, I built a bridge in Magdeburg and out of ten people from the East, nine people said that if they had a say in it, they wanted the wall back up again. Because for them it was secured work, a secured income, no pressure. The people from the East got the wrong impression of the West – they thought it was a paradise. But in fact, time is money and you have to work really hard. When the wall was up and you need a shovel, you don't have one, so you wait for it for two months, and for those two months you're playing cards, but for the same money. But at seven in the morning in the West, everything is there. When the wall got built, you could make a decision which side you wanted to jump. My mother, who was a young girl of fourteen, fifteen, jumped on the West side and said goodbye.

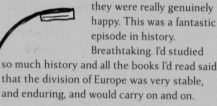

Biscuits

No TV-fest is complete without each Goggleboxer's preferred snacks and refreshments. Scarlett's dad, Mark, has very strong views about biscuits.

 Scarlett Moffatt: Bourbon biscuits shit all over custard creams, like.

 Mark Moffatt: Ginger nut is a proper man's biscuit.

 Scarlett Moffatt: How can you have a man biscuit?

 Mark Moffatt: If there was ever a man biscuit, it's a ginger nut.

 Scarlett Moffatt: Surely a man biscuit would be like a HobNob or something that's sturdy?

 Mark Moffatt: Can't get harder than a ginger nut.

Biscuit Hard-o-meter

TOUGH NUT

Ginger nut
'Man's biscuit'

HobNob
'Sturdy'

Bourbon
'Shits on Custard Creams'

Custard Cream
'Gets shat on by Bourbons'

SOGGY BISCUIT

Brian Cox

The almost literal heir to David Attenborough, the boyish ex-D:Ream keyboardist, Lancastrian particle physicist and nerd pin-up now officially owns space, time, gravity, science, the universe, life and atheism.

 Chris: What is it, Brian…? I always forget his name.

 Stephen: Funny that. You've had enough of 'em.

Brian Cox Fun Fact

Brian Cox got a D in his A-level maths exam.

Carolyne Michael: Britain's got so much talent.

Britain's Got Talent

SATURDAY, 7.30PM

ITV By overwhelming consensus 'better' than the similarly Simon Cowell-dictated star factory *The X Factor*, this is the talent show that shines equal limelight on dancers, jugglers and dogs as on aerobic karaoke singers.

 Carolyne Michael: Britain's got so much talent.

 Tom Malone: I like this because you get the real weirdos. I love all that. It's the same with *The X Factor* when all the loonpots come on.

 Tom Malone Jnr: That's the best bit. As soon as it gets to the live shows, Louis's are the only acts worth watching because they're all still crackpots, aren't they?

 Tom Malone: They all get doctored so they all sing the same way. It gets hard work; it's too serious.

 Leon: You know my opinion of Simon Cowell.

 June: He's supposed to be very good to work for. He's very generous.

 Leon: He's still a twat.

 Steph: I want Amanda's hairdresser.

 Dom: I want Amanda.

 Scarlett Moffatt: It's not *Britain's Got Talent* if someone doesn't have a sob story.

 Umar Siddiqui: It's called *Britain's Got Talent*, not *Britain's Got Talent and Emotional Issues.*

 Steph: Can you imagine the interview process? 'Have you had any shit happen to you; dead parents? Give us the worst shit and then you might be worth putting out.'

 Jenny: What do you think I could go up on stage and do?

 Lee: Sweep.

Watching
BRITAIN'S GOT TALENT
with THE TAPPERS

 The threshold of the Tapper house in north London is the first I cross in my *Gogglebox* odyssey, and I do so gingerly. I'm here to see them being filmed and am requested to put on a pair of those blue, *CSI*-style shoe covers. When the camera crew are tramping in and out, the floors must be protected. It's my first taste of the practical reality behind the reality show.

I spend most of the evening upstairs in Josh's bedroom, where the control booth is temporarily set up. It's a surreal experience watching the Tappers on a monitor watching *The Island with Bear Grylls* downstairs, live and unedited.

> "
> Jonathan Tapper:
> ### *There's too many cushions.*
> "

I return two weeks later, when normal service has resumed, and they've taken delivery of a brand-new grey leather suite, festooned with shiny silver and pink cushions. (They had to wait until the series was over for continuity.) 'There's too many cushions,' bemoans dad Jonathan, 48, back from the takeaway after a long day's chauffeuring for an executive car service. 'They look lovely, but I'm not sure about the colour.'

'You need to sit back on these couches,' instructs house-proud Nikki, 42, a nursery teacher. 'Because of the back support.' She looks around the room and then comments, 'We've got to get rid of those tables; they get on my nerves.' She's discovering that installing something new makes existing fixtures look old. 'Those tables are lovely,' protests Jonathan. 'They'll be sold by next week,' she promises, before calling the kids down.

It is with great speed that I am made part of this convivial and engulfing family as placemats and coasters are arranged at the dining table and Coke and water poured in preparation for an exhibition tournament of ribs, Chinese beef, spicy chicken, rice, stir-fried vegetables and salad, with a burger for Josh, 18, who sat an exam today. Pushed on how well it went, he says he doesn't really care about the subject. 'I do politics, economics, psychology and maths,' he tells me. 'And the only one I really like is politics.' His proud dad confirms: 'He loves politics. I don't like politicians. It's been my pet hate for years and years. And my son, bless him, wants to be a politician. Maybe he'll be one of the good ones.' Amy, 15, still in her school uniform and prone to making announcements like a mini town crier, declares, 'He just watches Victoria Derbyshire every day!'

Nikki is somewhat distracted at this point by the fact that her hair won't dry. 'It's still damp. I can't bear wet hair,' she complains. Jonathan then reminds her that she's wearing wet-look mousse. He turns back to his son. 'What about TV production, Joshie? You still interested in that?' he enquires. 'Yeah,' Josh replies. 'But this isn't a careers interview.'

They change the subject to a six-second clip of them that's 'gone viral' on the video-sharing service Vine. Titled 'The Biggest Lie on British Television', it's this exchange between Nikki and Josh:

Josh Tapper: It's basically a porno.

Nikki Tapper: It's not really, Josh. Have you seen a porno?

Josh Tapper: No.

And then he grins, in close-up. At last count, the Vine had racked up 2,193,507 loops, 1,342 likes, 920 shares and 37.2K tweets.

But the Tappers are a foursome whose lively, tactile affection for one another can no more be measured in 'likes' than put on for the cameras. It's part of the familial furniture. There is, as they say, a lot of love in the room ... up to a point. 'So annoying, those bloody cushions,' Jonathan grumbles. Feeling rather privileged to help christen their magnificent monument to sitting, I throw myself at the back support between Jonathan and Amy and get ready to sit in armchair judgement of *Britain's Got Talent*. We are still at the judges' auditions stage, with Cowell, David Walliams, Alesha Dixon and Amanda Holden in session.

Nikki Tapper: It's better than *The X Factor*.

> **Jonathan Tapper:**
> ## *So annoying, those bloody cushions.*

Jonathan Tapper: I think *Britain's Got Talent* appeals to a wider audience. *X Factor* now only appeals to people who are into that kind of singing. *Britain's Got Talent*, anybody can sit down to enjoy it. (pause) A very tight dress Amanda Holden's wearing there.

Nikki Tapper: She's gorgeous.

Josh Tapper: Simon's my favourite judge. I think he's a bit of a genius.

A pierced, long-haired, unemployed expectant dad, Aaron Marshall, 20, mounts the stage. Amanda Holden squeals with anticipation when she hears the opening bars of 'Let It Go' from Frozen, a penchant for which she is mocked in Britain's Got Talent circles, but she is in for a rude awakening.

Nikki Tapper: She's getting so excited.

The contestant lurches into a sort of death-metal version of the Disney singalong, dredging up a rasping, satanic vocal from the pits of his guts.

Nikki Tapper: A proper nutcase.

He is, unsurprisingly, buzzed off by Holden after two bars, but the other judges let her suffer by holding back.

Jonathan Tapper: He's just a weirdo.

Josh Tapper: It might have been a dare. I reckon Simon just got someone to come in off the street, just to annoy Amanda.

Nikki Tapper: Simon's laughing because she loves *Frozen* and she's gutted. But in a minute he's gonna get pissed off.

The Tappers explode into laughter as the audience join in with the song.

Jonathan Tapper: I saw the trailer but I never saw the film.

Nikki Tapper: What does Alesha look like? It's revealing, that top.

Jonathan Tapper: She hasn't even got nice boobs.

Nikki Tapper: She hasn't got any boobs. She's got very skinny, hasn't she?

Dixon leads an ironic standing ovation.

Jonathan Tapper: Oh, sit down, Alesha!

Holden says to the sore-throated wannabe, 'I really hope you lose your voice this afternoon.'

Jonathan Tapper: Ooh, that's a bit harsh. It's shit, but that's harsh.

Josh Tapper: I love Simon and David's bromance. I love the way he winds Simon up.

> "
>
> Josh Tapper:
>
> ### I love Simon and David's bromance.
>
> "

The contestant gets an ironic 'YES' from Walliams, Cowell and Dixon, and a 'big, fat, cold, icy, frozen NO' from Holden. She calls him 'the destroyer of Disney'.

Jonathan Tapper: It's so contrived!

A quartet of singing Pollyannas called Misstasia, aged 22–24, who are 'here to spread some princess magic' and profess a love for 'all things princessy' simper onto the stage and sing something from The Little Mermaid.

Jonathan Tapper: Is this *Disney's Got Talent*?

Josh Tapper: They could get a contract from Disney and entertain kids.

Jonathan Tapper: They should be on *Pitch Perfect 3*.

Nikki Tapper: I love this song. They've got good Disney voices.

Amy Tapper: They should all be in outfits: one of them Cinderella, one of them Belle, one of them Elsa, one of them Snow White.

Nikki Tapper: Amanda's in her element.

Jonathan Tapper: You're in your element.

Nikki Tapper: There is something magical about Disney, though. I'm ready to go to Disney now!

> "
>
> Nikki Tapper:
>
> ***There is something magical about Disney.***
>
> "

The princesses have to wait while the artificial tension is cranked up before the 'YES/NO' judgement.

Jonathan Tapper: They've sang their praises, they got a standing ovation and they're waiting: 'Are they gonna say YES, are they gonna say NO?' Well, of course they're gonna say YES! But they wait.

Nikki Tapper: Would you want to go back in the Magic Kingdom when we go to Disney?

Amy Tapper: One hundred and fifty per cent! Are you joking?

Nikki Tapper: We went when they were younger, when Amy was five, Josh was seven, then again when Amy was eight and Josh was ten. We've been back to Florida but not to Orlando, so I think we're gonna go in the summer. It is literally like La-La Land. I was seventeen when I went for the first time.

It's 'YES' times four for Misstasia, by the way. Next, a nervous 'entertainer', Peter Lambert, 32, takes an age to get on his unicycle and requires a hand from presenter Ant. He's bound to end up being good. Jonathan busts a gut.

Jonathan Tapper: He's gonna fall off.

Nikki Tapper: Ant looks like he's lost weight. When's he getting married?

Jonathan Tapper: We're not worried about that, we're watching an act!

Nikki Tapper: If there's anybody we could meet, it would be Ant and Dec. Or Gary Barlow.

Lambert is juggling meat cleavers while spinning plates. A caption advises us not to try this at home. He's a hit in the room and the theatre.

Nikki Tapper: He's a complete lunatic.

Jonathan Tapper: He's a good juggler.

Josh Tapper: He's got a lot of energy.

—— 66 ——

Jonathan Tapper:

**I'm very camp.
I'm not gay.**

—— 99 ——

Then, apropos of nothing:

Nikki Tapper: Why do people who are camp not admit they're gay?

Josh Tapper: Not all camp people are gay, mum!

Jonathan Tapper: I'm very camp. I'm not gay.

Nikki Tapper: Oh, shut up.

Simon Cowell Fun Fact

Simon Cowell allegedly loves the colour black so much that, according to his biographer, Tom Bower, he even insists on luxury black toilet roll.

Jonathan Tapper: I'm so camp I buy my clothes in Millets.

The climax comes with Old Men Grooving, a quintet of over-forties craftily dressed older than that in slacks, cardies and jumpers, who dummy the audience with an Astaire-style intro, then bodyswerve into an athletic routine to modern-ish toons by the Sugarhill Gang, James Brown and Yolanda Be Cool.

Jonathan Tapper: That guy in blue, he's not that old. They're not that old – forties, fifties?

Amy Tapper: They have children and grandchildren, I don't think they would have come on if they were going to embarrass themselves.

Nikki Tapper: Look at the trousers they're wearing! This is just class.

Jonathan Tapper: Their timing is very good. And you don't expect it.

Nikki Tapper: And their whole image with the outfits.

Jonathan Tapper: That guy looks like Shaun the Dark Destroyer in *The Chase*.

They bring the house down.

Jonathan Tapper: They're knackered now, look.

Back to hand-wringing about Alesha Dixon's weight.

Jonathan Tapper: Her neck is disgusting. It's like a man's neck.

BRITAIN'S GOT TALENT TV BINGO

Simon interrupting an act	David Walliams flirting with a man	Amanda saying she likes something Simon doesn't
A contestant with a sad backstory	Camera cutting to Ant and Dec looking astonished at side of stage	An uncomfortable-looking dog!
Camera cutting to audience member looking sceptical	A small boy being thrown into the air	Someone whose appearance makes you think they'll be rubbish actually being really good

Nikki Tapper: When she did *Strictly Come Dancing*, she was perfect.

Jonathan Tapper: Much more curvy.

Nikki Tapper: That's a good enough reason not to be in the public eye. If you're a singer or an actress, you're just not allowed to eat. Terrible, actually.

Jonathan Tapper: (returning to a theme) Why do they wait for the fourth 'YES'? If they've got three, they're through anyway!

It's difficult to leave the Tapper house. I blame the all-engulfing new sofa, which rather insists that you remain seated for ever. And I am somewhat weighted down with takeaway and hospitality. When I eventually leave, Jonathan has started to side with the waiting cab driver, and Nikki's hair is still wet.

Britney Spears

People in the public eye cause all manner of debate among our Goggleboxers. Former pop princess turned shaven-headed car crash Britney Spears comes under the focus of our eagle-eyed stars …

Britney Spears Fun Fact

In 2013, it was reported that British naval officers were playing Britney's music in an attempt to scare off pirates along the east coast of Africa.

 Sandra: G'wan Britney, let me see you … She's fat.

 Nikki Tapper: She's quite round in the bottom. But I'd like to look like that.

 Jonathan Tapper: I'd also like you to look like that.

GOGGLEBOX TV

Featuring
THE LETTER 'C'

Including
CATS
CHARLES AND DIANA'S WEDDING
CHILDBIRTH
THE COMMONWEALTH

Plus
COLONIC IRRIGATION
COUNTDOWN
CRUFTS

EXCLUSIVE! Watching Countdown with Leon & June!

Mr Tabby

Bliss

Gogglecats

The living rooms of Gogglebox are surprisingly bereft of feline company, considering how a snoozing cat on a sofa has been scientifically proven to enhance a room on a property show or a furniture showroom advert.

Leon and June used to have cats, but not anymore. Tom Malone Jnr holds the debatable view that cats have 'evil eyes'. And Chris's doughty old-timer, Ginge, 16, is rarely seen onscreen. (His younger, wilder housemate, Sherbet, never.)

Thank heavens, then, for the Woerdenwebers in the Wirral, who are outnumbered by multifarious moggies five to three, many of which at least ignore the limelight even if they don't seek it out. A continuity nightmare for *Gogglebox* editors they may be, but it's pleasing sport for viewing cat-fanciers to trace the Woerdenweber kitties' relocation around the monumental corner suite's hotspots and choice of laps.

For the record, the short-haired tabby-and-white is called Shadow, the short-haired black-and-white is Sybella (or Sybs), the luxurious long-haired tabby is, helpfully, Mr Tabby (or Tab), the equally long-haired tabby-and-black is Mer Imbrium (or Imbri), which translates

as 'sea on the Moon', and finally there's the grumpy long-haired white-and-tortoiseshell Bliss, a rescue cat with a dicky eye. (When she first arrived, the boys started spraying, because they didn't like her, but hairball harmony has since been achieved.) Some of them wander outdoors, sheltering in inclement weather under a gazebo which seems to have been erected on the patio just for them. Mr Tabby still comes in glistening with raindrops on his magisterial tawny fur, however.

Eve reveals that she wants a Rottweiler. If the household took a democratic vote on *that* proposed addition to the household, you suspect it would be vetoed by a show of paws.

Shadow

> ❝
>
> **Tom Malone Jnr holds the debatable view that cats have 'evil eyes'.**
>
> ❞

Sybella

Ginge

Mer Imbrium (Imbri)

Through the power of TV, we take you back to 1981

Charles and Diana's Wedding

In a pre-cynicism era of British history, a prince married a lady and made her a princess at St Paul's Cathedral with a global guest list of 750 million. What could possibly go wrong?

We sit and watch news footage of the 'wedding of the century'. For some of us, it brings back fairy-tale memories. For others, it's all a bit puzzling.

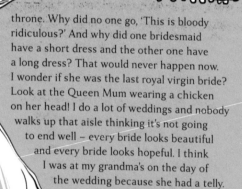

 Rev. Kate: What's weird about this is that nobody's got their mobiles out. No one's filming it on their iPhone. The dress is creased to hell, isn't it? It's bonkers. What scares me about this now is how young she was and how we thought it was OK. She's nineteen and she's marrying a man who's nearly forty.

He was thirty-two.

 Rev. Kate: Well, she was only nineteen and she's marrying the heir to the throne. Why did no one go, 'This is bloody ridiculous?' And why did one bridesmaid have a short dress and the other one have a long dress? That would never happen now. I wonder if she was the last royal virgin bride? Look at the Queen Mum wearing a chicken on her head! I do a lot of weddings and nobody walks up that aisle thinking it's not going to end well – every bride looks beautiful and every bride looks hopeful. I think I was at my grandma's on the day of the wedding because she had a telly. It was a 90-mile journey.

 Jenny: That frock – bloody awful. It was too much. Like something out of *Dynasty*. That's one of them dresses you'd wear if you were pregnant, getting married.

 Lee: Creased to f**k.

 Jenny: Fergie's dress was beautiful. Diana's dress has stuck in the door – she's like Madonna. It was a bit rushed, wasn't it? Didn't she have, like, a rehearsal? How did she know she could walk with it? I didn't think her hair looked very nice either.

 Lee: Look at the bridesmaids' dresses!

 Jenny: Actually, if Charles had a trendy haircut, he'd be nice-looking.

 Mark Moffatt: (to Scarlett) You were minus nine.

 Scarlett Moffatt: How did he pull her?

 Betty Moffatt: It was family-arranged.

 Mark Moffatt: She was good breeding stock.

 Betty Moffatt: I was only eleven at the time but I remember all the hype around the dress. The train! Look at the size of it. It's like a *My Big Fat Gypsy Wedding* dress.

 Scarlett Moffatt: She looks like a princess. I think she'd approve of Kate now. And it's nice that they've given Charlotte her name as well.

 Mark Moffatt: No one beats us for pomp and pageantry.

 Betty Moffatt: She didn't look very happy, did she?

Scarlett Moffatt: You'd think she'd be smiling – it's the happiest day of her life.

Mark Moffatt: You need a bus to get to the altar.

Scarlett Moffatt: Or rollerskates. Are you crying?

Betty Moffatt: No, I'm not crying.

Mary: Giles and I had just started going out, and we were both shocked by the shooting of John Lennon at the end of 1980. We suddenly had the wind taken out of our sails about being non-stuffy. And then with this royal wedding, we welcomed the return of stuffiness and formality and order again. It was a return to wholesomeness, whereas the whole John Lennon world had gone a bit dark. We were Beatles fans.

Giles: The Beatles enhanced our lives. Now people don't listen to the music in the same way we did; they're not as attentive. We were amazed. I mean, *The White Album*, my sister and I would sit for hours listening to 'Revolution No. 9', waiting for Yoko to say that rude bit. When I was at school, I got very into progressive rock. The big thing was having the concept album, King Crimson, Emerson, Lake and Palmer, opening the thing, looking at the artwork, going 'Wow!' and then putting on the headphones. Totally inward. We are very anti-drugs now. I'm very anti-skunk.

Julie Malone: Here we go, lamb to the slaughter.

Tom Malone Jnr: I've got the five-pound coin from this.

Tom Malone: He's kinky, Charles, to have turned his back on her to go and get Camilla. He's proper got kinky tastes.

Shaun Malone: I hate this kind of stuff, me. Why is it people get married on TV? And people having kids. It really pisses me off.

Tom Malone Jnr: That carriage is like Mary Poppins's bag.

Julie Malone: It was the Emanuels who designed that dress.

Tom Malone Jnr: Who are the Emanuels?

Julie Malone: Designers.

Tom Malone Jnr: They sound like the Mexican Jackson 5.

Tom Malone: Has she shown her face yet? It could be anybody walking up there.

Julie Malone: She's so slim.

Tom Malone: She could be 18 stone underneath that dress.

Julie Malone: Poor girl.

Tom Malone: He was proper punching above his weight.

Shaun Malone: Same as William.

Tom Malone: Looks like she's walking to the gallows.

Julie Malone: She was.

Tom Malone: I love a good organ playing.

Tom Malone Jnr: There's no need for the aisle to be that long – just get a wider church.

Nikki Tapper: Aaah. This is nice.

Josh Tapper: But neither of them liked each other, so why is it nice?

Nikki Tapper: It was nice at the time.

Jonathan Tapper: I was fourteen.

 Nikki Tapper: I will never ever forget watching this. I was eight.

 Jonathan Tapper: This was massive around the world at the time, Josh, because the world loved Diana. Do you remember David Emanuel who was on *I'm a Celebrity*? It was him who designed the dress.

 Nikki Tapper: She was beautiful, though. She looks so happy.

 Jonathan Tapper: Well, it's not every day you become a princess, is it?

 Nikki Tapper: Kate is beautiful but she was in a league of her own.

 Josh Tapper: Isn't Kate's wedding a bit nicer than this wedding, because we know that William and Kate actually love each other?

 Jonathan Tapper: In that respect, yes.

 Amy Tapper: I'm really confused. Who's Camilla?

 Jonathan Tapper: His wife now.

 Nikki Tapper: Was Kate a virgin?

 Jonathan Tapper: Course she wasn't. They've changed the rules, haven't they? You weren't allowed to marry a divorced woman then and become king. But Charles can now.

 Nikki Tapper: Look at this aisle, kids. Look at Anne.

 **Jonathan Tapper:** Look at Margaret.

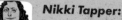 **Nikki Tapper:** Princess Margaret used to come to my school, Haberdashers' Aske's; she's a patron.

 Jonathan Tapper: Princess Margaret. She's in a cerise colour.

 Leon: Of course, he was a bastard. He was having an affair! He only married her to provide children.

 June: They got married in St Paul's, not Westminster Abbey, and that broke with tradition. She was a child, really, and naive in many ways, I think. It was all a bit nursery rhyme-ish. Compare Diana's dress to Kate's.

 Leon: It's a sensible marriage, Kate and William's.

 June: They're a similar age, they've been to university together.

 Leon: He's not as funny looking as Charles.

 June: The Emanuels were quite unknown then.

 Chris: I used to have a little tiny book they gave me at school. It had Charles and Diana on it.

 Stephen: Back then, we thought she looked beautiful, but that dress is hideous.

 Chris: God, look at it. It's just ridiculous!

Stephen: But very royal. Kate's was a bit plain compared to that. That's what we wanna see. Maybe not so meringue-y, but…

Chris: I bet it was bloody heavy, though.

Stephen: She liked a bit of Asian, didn't she? Dodi Fayed. He was Asian-ish. The Pakistani doctor – he was a good-looking fella.

Chris: We all like a bit of Asian.

Stephen: They should never have married. She's like a breeding cow with a prize bull. Look at the Queen Mother, she was an old bag, wasn't she?

Andrew Michael: I didn't watch it at the time and I'd rather not watch it now. This is the first time I've seen it.

Carolyne Michael: We were all so disappointed. It was such a shit dress.

Louis Michael: Is the dress controlling the woman?

Carolyne Michael: Kate Middleton's was much nicer. She had the world to choose from and she chose that. It's exactly the wedding dress you'd have drawn when you were a child and that's what she did. We're exactly the same age, me and Diana, so I always took a very close interest. He wanted his nice little virgin, who he thought he could mould, and, of course, he chose the wrong virgin.

Sid Siddiqui: What a day that was. It was a whole-day thing on the television.

Baasit Siddiqui: Why does it have to be a white dress and so long? It must be so dirty.

Sid Siddiqui: Who would have decided on the length of the dragging bit? Is it some royal protocol?

Baasit Siddiqui: You can hear the band getting tired.

Sid Siddiqui: The Queen Mother was much younger before it started.

Umar Siddiqui: Those two bridesmaids holding the end of the train are in a different time zone. It's the eighties, isn't it? It's all about big fashion.

Baasit Siddiqui: It's weird watching this and knowing what's in her future.

Sandra: That was 1981. Do you know why I remember that? Because my son was one. I didn't know about Camilla at that time, but I won't lie, I wasn't really into Diana; I was into Fergie, because I saw a documentary about her. I had the clippings of her sucking the toe. Their scandal fascinated me. I was into the bad part of the royals! But I loved Diana's dress. But Charles had a little scam going on, innit? But it's alright, though – he loved Camilla, what can we do? He was good-looking, he was young, he had brown hair!

Ralf Woerdenweber: This was all over the television in Germany. Germany stopped, Vivienne, seriously. The streets were empty.

Viv Woerdenweber: I had to work. I was a veterinary nurse and the vet didn't close, so I sat and watched it with tea and biscuits at work. That dress is in a museum at Althorp.

Ralf Woerdenweber: How long was the train? Eight metres? The walk down the aisle is probably one and a half miles.

Viv Woerdenweber: So many people went to the wedding they couldn't fit them all into Westminster Abbey and that's why it was at St Paul's.

Ralf Woerdenweber: His ears are so big, Spock from the Enterprise is jealous of him.

Eve Woerdenweber: She looks like she's walking to her own funeral.

Childbirth

The miracle of birth comes up surprisingly frequently with the Goggleboxers, though they all have very different takes on it.

Louis Michael: A human birth is the most vile, disgusting thing I have ever seen.

Josef: If nature had done things properly, instead of having this messy arrangement and pain for the mother, you'd do the same as you'd do with chickens. Lay an egg, nice and simple, and put it in the airing cupboard for nine months.

Stephen: Thank the Lord I was not born a woman. Would you want to go through that?

Chris: No, I bloody wouldn't.

Jenny: I gave the same advice my mother gave me: 'It'll be the hardest day's work you ever do in your life, but it'll be the most rewarding.'

Sandra: My third and fourth: 'No way, I'm not pushing out nuttin. Take it out yourself.'

Leon: I remember you being wheeled out, and saying, 'Look,' and there was Helen.

June: And what did you say? 'Ooh, she looks just like a little monkey.'

Louis Michael: A human birth is the most vile, disgusting thing I have ever seen.

Andrew Michael: I remember when you were born, Katy. I put you on my shoulder and you didn't move. Whereas with Louis, he was bouncing off.

Louis Michael: Yeah, I've been trying to get away from you from day one!

Rev. Kate: I swore at the midwife, I swore at you.

Graham: You called me a flipping plonker.

Rev. Kate: I called you a lot worse than that.

The Commonwealth

Officially an intergovernmental organization of fifty-three member states around the world, who swim, bounce and run against each other every four years like there's still a bit of a British Empire. Or ...

66

Stephen:

It's all the countries we own, that we raped and pillaged and stole.

99

Colonic Irrigation

Jenny explains to Lee how this complementary therapy works, in her own inimitable fashion.

Jenny: It's basically like a massive eme... emem. Like an enema. An enema.

Lee: I don't know what that is.

Jenny:

They stick it up your bum to clean it out. And they put it through a machine and you can see it going by.

Lee:

What? Like The Generation Game?

CUDDLY TOY?

Leon: All I can get is piss.

Countdown

THURSDAY, 2.10PM

CH4 The first programme ever to air on the newborn 'fourth channel' in 1982 – and it's still counting down thirty seconds to that iconic 'Boo!' while clever contestants do anagrams and sums and fail to impress even cleverer female hostesses. These days it's presented by ex-*Apprentice* henchman Nick Hewer.

O I A S N H T S P

Tom Malone: Shaun picked an eight-letter word out on *Countdown* straight away. Because he's dyslexic he can see the letters. To him, all letters are jumbled up.

Shaun Malone: It's like an unfair advantage on *Countdown*.

Tom Malone Jnr: If you're going on *Countdown*, being dyslexic's sort of a superpower.

Baasit Siddiqui: If you got a high one early, you'd just sit there dancing to the music, wouldn't you?

Leon: Sin.

June: Passion.

Sandra: Fins. Pins.

Stephen: Shit.

Chris: Shits.

Leon: All I can get is piss.

Countdown Fun Fact

The only three words with consecutive sets of double letters are 'Bookkeeper' and 'Bookkeepers' and 'Tattooed'. (Thanks Bill.)

Watching
COUNTDOWN
with LEON AND JUNE

Leon and June are the nation's grand-parents. They have that grandparental habit of proudly listing their grand-children (Frances, 18; Sam, 16; Fay, 16).

Leon turned 80 this year and repose is his default position, but he jumps up to offer to make me a ham sandwich at their neat suburban Liverpool semi, which is based not far from where Paul McCartney and John Lennon grew up. June, a sprightly 78, combines a daily swim with *Countdown* to keep fit both physically and mentally. They are of a vintage where the short-

Leon:

If any party forms a coalition with UKIP, I'm going to New Zealand.

term memory is less robust than the long-term. Both forget things, but rely on the other to remember for them. 'Who was I raging about last night, June?' asks Leon from his reclining throne. 'Lorraine Kelly,' replies June from the kitchen. They are a collective intelligence.

Of all the fixed *Gogglebox* views, theirs is the most instantly recognizable: side by side, face on, in those straight-backed mushroom-coloured armchairs (actually, June's is one end of a sofa), divided only by a nest of mahogany tables, atop which is a framed photo of the grandkids. The biscuits and cafetière coffees go on a breakaway table – as does my ham sandwich. Attentive hosts, June and Leon are up and down a lot, which comes as something of a surprise given their advanced years.

Our time together is dominated by talk of the general election, which is only a few days away. The ex-teachers are stout socialists for whom tolerance is an article of faith that stops just short of Nigel Farage. 'If any party forms a coalition with UKIP,' states Leon, 'I'm going to New Zealand.' (One of their two daughters lives there.)

Though his vocal appreciation of the female form gets Leon into trouble, his ripe age positions it just the right side of 'incorrigible'. He does, after all, chiefly appraise the likes of *Countdown* boffin Rachel Riley and *Britain's Got Talent* judge Amanda Holden for the loveliness of their arms. A blue-blooded Everton fan, his actual vice is Sky Sports, which he watches on his own in the front room.

'Are you Jewish?' Leon asks me, with a frankness common to senior citizens. 'You could pass for Jewish,' he offers, by way of a compliment. Leon's Judaism means he sees something of his and June's rocky 1950s courtship in that of Jewish heir Atticus Aldridge and the Dowager Countess's great-niece Lady Rose on *Downton*. 'What are you doing, marrying a *shiksa*?' his parents apparently asked him at the time. That he 'loved her loads' was his reason for defying orthodoxy.

A hopeless romantic.

June: When I came to live in Liverpool it was Protestant/Catholic and I couldn't cope with it. I thought the one thing I wanted for my children is that they didn't grow up prejudiced. You don't like that person because of something they've done, but not because they're Scottish, or Welsh, or whatever. I said (to my daughters), 'You can marry anybody you like, except a Liverpool supporter!'

June, who retains her singsong Welsh Valleys accent despite thinking of herself as an adopted Liverpudlian ('Liverpool paid my wages'), takes nothing for granted. When she was in Salford for a *BBC Breakfast* interview, she noted that they were put up in the Holiday Inn, while their producer was relegated to the Holiday Inn Express. Leon, who only looks to be on the brink of dozing off once during my visit, is proud to tell me he gets his hair cut by Adele on Penny Lane. He's as likely to get a plaque there as the Beatles.

> "
> June (to her daughters):
>
> ### *You can marry anybody you like, except a Liverpool supporter!*
> "

Since retiring, they've been to New York, Washington, Boston, Vermont ('I sang "Moonlight in Vermont" to June as we crossed the border,' says Leon) and Virginia. But Leon's bucket list still contains Nashville. June, clearing away my plate, says to her adoring husband, 'If you're going there, I'm going to the Grand Canyon.'

Unable to sit between the reigning monarchs of *Gogglebox* without actually perching on the occasional table, I slot in next to June, whose copy of the *Radio Times* is ready to be turned into an ad hoc notepad, and we all get ready for a Tuesday edition of the indestructible, thirty-three-year-old teatime words/numbers quiz. Along with Nick Hewer, we also have Rachel Riley in the former Carol Vorderman role of highly educated hostess.

June: I used to go swimming, do a bit of shopping, come home, have a cup of tea and watch *Countdown*. That's my day: working the body, working the brain. I have a competition with myself. And Leon usually comes in at the end and ogles Rachel Riley. But now they've changed the time and we're missing it more. I like Nick Hewer.

Leon: He's a good socialist. I never liked Carol Vorderman. She didn't turn me on. I find Nick Hewer insufferable.

The theme music plays and we are off.

Leon: June's a big fan.

June: I try and get a seven-worder every week. I'm not normally a very competitive person, which is why Leon and I can't play bridge together.

Nick indulges in some pre-match repartee about Labradors with Rachel.

Leon: She's not as sexy today.

June: Disappointed, are you, Leon?

Leon: I love the eyes. Too young for me, of course.

June: She's got everything, that girl: brains, looks, personality.

One contestant is from Solihull.

June: Ooh, Solihull, Leon.

Leon: A friend of mine's daughter lives in Solihull.

Susie Dent's sidekick in Dictionary Corner is former pop singer and Classic FM DJ Myleene Klass, who's wearing glasses for the occasion.

June: She's looking very studious.

Leon: She's gorgeous. Didn't she have a nasty divorce?

June uses the back of the Radio Times to write down the letters as they are plucked.

Leon: Er … (trying to find a word from the letters) Read.

June: Swear? Nears?

Leon: Rude.

June: Re-warn?

The contestants offer a seven-letter word, 'wonders', and one eight-letter that's disqualified, 'wounders'.

Leon: She is gorgeous, Myleene Klass, even with big glasses on. Lovely arms. I like nice arms on a woman.

Letter round number two; the clock starts to tick down …

Leon: Read.

June: Tires.

The winning entry is a seven, 'loiters', trumped by Myleene's eight: 'godliest'. Time for the first numbers round.

June: You can train yourself to do these quite easily.
2 x 75 = 150. 5 x 5 = 25. 150 + 25 = 175. 175 − 3 = 172.

June is three off the required total, which we agree is not at all bad.

Leon: I never get these.

The teatime teaser is given for viewers to solve over the first ad break: NAILHIRE. The clue? 'It became a victim of the recession and never recovered'.

June: Gosh, that's hard.

Leon: I always get the rude ones.

June: Hairline. Recession, receding hair: brilliant!

Leon: She's a clever girl, my wife.

Round three, and Rachel pulls out a 'Z'.

Leon: Her legs are skinny.

June: Ooh, can you have 'nazal'? Oh no, that's with an 'S'. 'Manly'?

Leon: 'Manly' is good, June.

A six-letter wins it: 'namely'.

Leon: She is gorgeous, Myleene Klass.

June: She's an accomplished musician.

Round four.

Leon: Bog. Dog. Bite.

June: Can you have 'doges'? Hodge? Tides.

Leon: Shed.

The winning word is . . . 'ghosted'.

June: Ooh, well done. I only got a five.

Leon: Is Susie Oxbridge as well?

The Dictionary Corner duo play an eight-letter blinder with . . . 'gobshite'. It's described as 'vulgar slang'.

June: No! Nick's not happy about that.

Leon: That's all Liverpool supporters: gobshites.

More numbers.

June: Ooh, I'm not doing well on this one at all. I can't get it.

Leon: It's amazing the way they get it. They're quite good, these two. (distracted again) She's lovely, isn't she?

Round five: more letters. The clock ticks again.

June: Sacred.

> ## "
> Leon (on the bald man in the Money Supermarket advert):
>
> ### I hate this. This is appalling. I'd kick him up the backside. It's dreadful.
>
> "

I've got 'waisted'. Oops, I wasn't meant to be playing.

The contestants tie with 'waister' and 'waiters'. Dictionary Corner can only trump these with 'waisted'. Epic win! Round six.

Leon: Rachel was married, but she left him after fifteen months, I think.

June: Can you have 'Maori'? No, that's a capital 'M'.

Only a five from the contestants: 'minor'. Myleene suggests 'mohair'. June gets scribbling for the next numbers round.

June: $8 \times 25 \times 4 = 800. 9 - 1 = 8. 8 \times 4 = 32 \ldots$

June runs out of time. Rachel storms it, as is traditional.

Leon: That's amazing!

June: When we first watched it, we thought you had to use all the numbers and we could never get it right.

During the ads, we are assailed by that grotesque spectacle for Money Supermarket with the bald man welded to a lady's bottom half.

Leon: I hate this. This is appalling.

June: I usually go out and make tea or put the ironing away during the adverts.

Leon: I'd kick him up the backside. It's dreadful.

June: A lot of the people I go swimming with were talking about it, but none of them knew what the advert was for. Well, that's defeated the purpose.

The final part.

June: I usually have a writing pad. But I really am a back-of-an-envelope person.

Leon: (beginning to guess in the letters round) Pee. Post.

June: Stove.

The contestants have 'stove' and 'votes'; trumped, as ever, by Dictionary Corner, who have 'covets'.

The final round. But will June get the seven-letter word she always aims for on every Countdown?

Leon: Peer. Pear.

June: Praises. Yes! I got it! I'm happy now.

Time for the Countdown conundrum. We can't crack it; nor can the contestants. The answer is 'parchment'.

Leon: How old is Nick?

June: Is he seventy-two? I think they came in with a cake for his seventieth birthday. (she turns to me) Would you like a sandwich?

When we've totted up our scores and I've brushed the sandwich crumbs from my lap, it's time for me to reluctantly leave Leon and June. I only wish I could go back and do it all again next week.

Crufts

UK dog show established in 1886: still comparing hounds' teeth and sending their owners round obstacle courses in 2015.

June: They say we're a nation of dog lovers.

June: They say we're a nation of dog lovers.

Leon: I'm not.

Baasit Siddiqui: They're a nation of dog lovers in Britain. They love dogs in China, too. Just in a different way.

Umar Siddiqui: What's Crufts like in China? It's a cookery show.

Dom: You see, this is my problem with this sort of thing: how can you compare a golden retriever against a shih-tzu, against a this, that or the other, by feeling its bones and looking up its arse?

In 2015, a dog died at Crufts and the post-mortem showed several types of poison had been ingested.

Steph: Midsomer Crufts!

Tom Malone: What's going on? It's like the Russian mafia's getting into Crufts now!

GOGGLEBOX TV D

Featuring
THE LETTER 'D'

Including
THE DEATH OF DIANA (PRINCESS OF WALES)
DINOSAURS
DOCTOR WHO

Plus
DOGS
DOWNTON ABBEY

and
DRAGONS' DEN

EXCLUSIVE! The Goggleboxers remember Diana, Princess of Wales.

Through the power of TV, we take you back to 1997

The Death of Diana (Princess of Wales)

The opposite of a fairy-tale ending for the princess who divorced a prince and threatened to bring down the monarchy by going out with an Egyptian, Dodi Fayed: both were killed in a car crash in a Parisian tunnel in 1997. Conspiracy theorists suspected foul play; the world mourned. It was always sombre when I watched these clips with the Goggleboxers. Some of us remembered it well, others were too young, but there were always strong reactions to the footage.

Rev. Kate: That's still shocking, isn't it? We were at my mum and dad's and we turned on the telly while we were getting ready to go to church. You watch it now, and because we know the rest of the story, we go: 'Don't get in a car with a drunk driver and no seatbelt on.' This was Tony Blair's defining moment. He must have been bricking it. We still liked him then: he hadn't fluffed it up at that point. When I watch that now, I say: 'Tony, don't take us to war! Tony!' That was when Tony Blair was still an Anglican. Before he converted to Roman Catholicism. He was High Anglican, anyway, so that was his preference: bells and smells, and doffing and bobbing. And his wife's Roman Catholic, and his kids, and I think while he was prime minister he didn't feel able to convert.

 Jenny: We was in Chester – where were you?

 Lee: The newsreader in the morning was filling up.

 Mark Moffatt: I remember a few weeks before she died, she was getting slated in the papers.

 Betty Moffatt: But that's what we do, we build people up to pull them to bits, then build them back up again.

 Scarlett Moffatt: Didn't she have her boobs out?

 Mark Moffatt: No, that'll be Fergie.

 Scarlett Moffatt: I had a dance-medal test, because it was a Sunday, and I remember going down and they had the telly in the passage and everyone was watching it. Nanny rang you in the morning.

 Mark Moffatt: You couldn't have the future King of England's mother married to a Muslim. Not when he's the head of the Church of England.

 Betty Moffatt: It was sad because she'd finally found happiness, hadn't she?

 Scarlett Moffatt: People were sobbing their hearts out. It wasn't as if it was someone actually in their family.

 Jonathan Tapper: I reckon there's only a handful of people that really know what happened.

 Nikki Tapper: I remember phoning your mum, because she loved her.

 Stephen: I come out of a club, I was walking through Vauxhall and someone shouted out, 'Your princess, she's dead!'

 Baasit Siddiqui: All I remember that day is that there was nothing else on TV.

 Sandra: She must be vexed that she's not here to f**k up Camilla.

> 66
>
> Betty Moffatt:
>
> **It was sad because she'd finally found happiness, hadn't she?**
>
> 99

Mary: It was a strange time when that mass hysteria took hold in that first week. Even Giles and I went to Kensington Palace.

 Giles: We got sucked in.

 Mary: We didn't lay a wreath because we couldn't bear the waste of all the polythene.

 Giles: No, we brought some country flowers. I remember it was really bad weather the day we went, really squally summer weather. Everybody was really upset, completely out of proportion.

 Mary: We watched the funeral on the black-and-white set in the front room. We thought with a black-and-white set you won't bother to watch it unless it's really interesting. On a colour set, you can watch anything. I remember watching it with our two daughters, and I remember hearing that people were upset when Chairman Mao died, because they were used to seeing his face come on every day. And in the same way, we were all upset about Di. It was terrible. She was so young.

 Giles: The conspiracy theories whizzing around that event are almost irresistible.

 Mary: I don't think it was an Establishment plot.

 Giles: She was a loose cannon, and the royal family didn't want her going out with Dodo – what's he called? The Harrods man. It's quite compelling.

 Mary: We had to go to a wedding on the day of the funeral and we thought it would be cancelled, but it wasn't. I thought the single most moving thing about the whole event was the five royal men walking down the Mall behind the coffin and not crying. Their composure was so admirable. Whereas the mob was sobbing.

 Giles: Inconsolable. It was a turning point, the 'Dianafication' of Britain, when people started to emote rather than being a buttoned-up nation.

> "
>
> Ralf Woerdenweber:
>
> **I miss her smile. She had to die because she didn't fit into the picture. She was loved all over the world.**
>
> "

 Mary: Elton John started it when he started confessing he had bulimia. I think Di rather took her cues from him.

 Julie Malone: I woke up that night. We'd been out. And for some reason I woke up and went downstairs and made a cup of tea, something I don't usually do. And you came downstairs to see where I was. It was heartbreaking. We lived in Chorley Road when this happened.

 Tom Malone: The S-280 was supposed to be the safest car on the road, but it didn't do them any good, did it? I don't think they ever tied down that little white Fiat that was involved, did they?

 Nikki Tapper: I thought I was going to go into labour with Josh that day. I was at home in bed, and I'm glad I didn't. I didn't want to have a baby that day. It was a bad day.

 Amy Tapper: I reckon it was the driver.

Nikki Tapper: I think it went wrong. I don't think she was meant to get killed, I think Dodi was meant to go. It was too horrific, too random and too extreme not to have been planned.

 Josef: I have no idea where I was when Diana died.

 Bill: I was in bed. It was a Sunday. The news is never allowed to happen on a Sunday.

 Leon: I am convinced that the royal family and MI5 had a part in that.

 June: Tony Blair looks like Michael Sheen, doesn't he? We'd been to a wedding the day before. My daughter told me there'd been a terrible car accident and I thought she meant somebody from the wedding.

 Carolyne Michael: Louis was just a baby, and I remember coming downstairs and putting on the television. I was in total shock.

 Andrew Michael: She was a modern goddess.

 Carolyne Michael: And that's why she was sacrificed. There was a pagan temple under that tunnel and she hit the thirteenth pillar.

 Louis Michael: WHAT?!

 Andrew Michael: She challenged the House of Windsor's supremacy.

 Sid Siddiqui: I remember this, it was a Sunday, because it was your mum's birthday. This is the one where a newscaster cries, isn't it? I think what Tony Blair said came from the heart. I well up listening to him. It's raw emotion.

 Sandra: I cried when she died and all that.

 Sandy: I was in Cornwall. We went and stayed in a cottage. Everybody else was sleeping, but I got up for a cup of tea, came downstairs and just switched on the telly. And it was on. I just broke down! I went screaming around the house! 'Wake up, wake up, wake up!'

 Sandra: I went out that night, and I was coming in that morning with my friend Julie, from a dance, drunk as a skunk. Not heavily drunk, but we were mashed up. I heard the news, I think we must have cried for ourselves, and cried for her. Emotions were all in the air. It was sad she'd gone and left two boys, but that's how God done it, man.

 Sandy: She's got two lovely boys, and now a lovely granddaughter. They've got her genes and I see everything they do Diana would like. She'll never be forgotten.

 Sandra: You know what? If she hadn't gone, there'd be some problems, still, though. If that Harrods baby had come true and he was a different colour… How old would he be now?

If you mean the rumours that Diana was pregnant by Dodi Fayed, son of Harrods owner Mohamed Al-Fayed? He or she would be seventeen.

 Sandra: That's when the black roots is coming in!

 Sandy: They might start to change! Little George might find himself a little ting! It's a new generation, babes.

 Viv Woerdenweber: It was terrible.

 Ralf Woerdenweber: These days, thirty seconds later it would have been all over Twitter, Facebook, all over the place.

 Viv Woerdenweber: Tony Blair gave a really good speech.

Dinosaurs

 Alex Michael: Why would you be afraid of dinosaurs?

 Carolyne Michael: Because they killed us.

 Alex Michael: No, they didn't kill us.

Carolyne Michael: Well, they could do.

Doctor Who

SATURDAY, 7.30PM

BBC1 Eternally regenerative family-friendly science-fiction franchise which has defined every generation since 1963 and staged a superhuman comeback after a nine-year sabbatical, emerging stronger, more popular, more profitable and more Welsh.

Ralf Woerdenweber: You have to be a child or stoned to understand it. Or English.

Doctor Who Fun Fact

The distinctive sound of the Tardis appearing was created by dragging a set of house keys across the bass strings of a piano and playing the resulting sound backwards.

 Ralf Woerdenweber: You have to be a child or stoned to understand it. Or English.

 Dom: How do they eat? Have you ever seen a Dalek whip up an omelette?

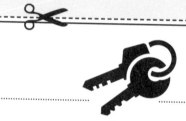

> Steph:
>
> ***I bet they don't know how to do a Bloody Mary either.***

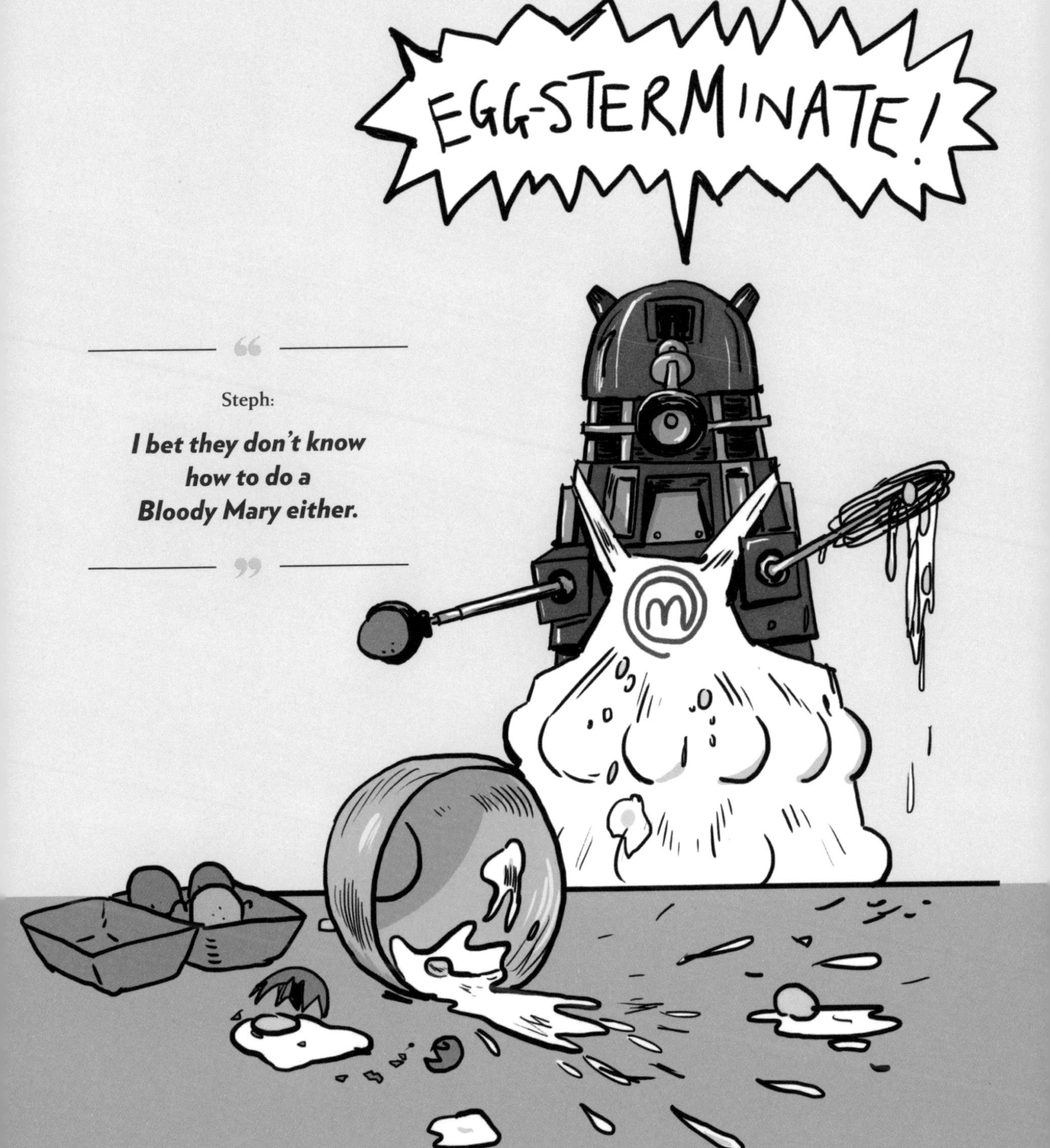

DAVE

The Malones

IZZY

The Malones

LUCY

The Malones

FRANKIE

The Malones

GOGGLE DOGS

BOBBY

The Malones

BUSTER

Rev. Kate & Graham

HARRY

Scarlett Moffatt

GIGI

Steph & Dom

The cats of Gogglebox total six. At nine, dogs outnumber them and certainly outweigh them, thanks to the Malones' four Rottweilers and one Staffordshire bull terrier who allow the family to share their house in Manchester. A critic once observed that ex-WWF-wrestler-turned-film-star Dwayne 'The Rock' Johnson 'looks bigger than whichever vehicle he just stepped out of', and the same would be true if you saw the four-legged Malones barrel out of that famous front room.

They're taken out for a walk, or run, at night, wearing flashing collars, 'when everybody else has gone', explains Tom. 'Even though they're dead soft, some people are a bit wary of them.' Between them, they have churned the back lawn into mud and turned the back room where they decompress and wipe their feet before re-entering polite society into 'a drying-off room'. But they are indeed dead soft and any one of them might fall asleep on your feet with their belly in the air. Once a month, the Malones hire a carpet cleaner.

Dave is what they call 'a size-zero Rottweiler, he's so skinny; he's the only dog that can play fetch with himself'. He's lovingly described as 'an idiot with a big heart' and his record is five bones in his mouth at once. Frankie, the scarred Staffie, is a rescue dog who'd been on the RSPCA website in Gloucester for nearly two years. The inseparable girls, chunky Izzy and ringleader Lucy, were rejected by their mother at four weeks, 'so we took them under our wing, and kind of kept them'. Bob the puppy's not yet a year old. Until you've been to the bathroom at the top of the stairs and had all five of them follow you, you haven't lived.

The Mancunian pooches made an immediate impact from series four, and quickly joined their modest Kent cousin Squidge and outstretched Notts counterpart Buster in *Gogglebox* iconography. Of those other dogs,

> 66
>
> ## The cats of **Gogglebox** total six. At nine, dogs outnumber them and certainly outweigh them, thanks to the Malones' four Rottweilers and one Staffordshire bull terrier.
>
> 99

Steph and Dom's sausage dog actually behaves more like a cat, coiling herself up into a short-haired cushion and ignoring the lubricated mayhem going on around her, patiently humouring her parents by joining in the occasional dance to Dire Straits.

Meanwhile, Buster, the retired greyhound who shares the vicarage and the couch with Reverend Kate and her husband, Graham, turns six this year. He is tattooed inside his ear, like all working greyhounds. When his trainer declined to euphemistically 'retire' him after two years' work, he gave Buster a new life via the Retired Greyhound Trust charity, through which Kate and Graham adopted him. Buster never actually raced, it turns out; 'He can't corner,' Graham explains. Greyhounds, though large, make perfect pets: they're happy on their own, have no genetic deformities due to breeding, and, Kate proudly reports, 'have no dog odour!' We shall gloss over Buster's early reputation for reclining on his back and confirming his gender, and marvel instead at the way he leaps up onto the *Gogglebox* sofa as soon as the cameras arrive and takes his position, like a true pro. Sometimes in *that* position.

It's sheer coincidence that Kate contrasts Buster, favourably, to a basset hound in terms of his fragrance. 'The smell of a basset hound will take the back of your throat off!' she warns. Although as yet camera-shy, it transpires that Chris in Brighton has recently invited a gorgeous basset into his bungalow: Fred, who's owned by Chris's boyfriend. 'He needs a bloody bath,' sniffs Stephen.

No such problems for Harry, the Moffatts' attentively groomed shih-tzu, with his hair tied into a neat topknot, who is often seen grappling with ankles on the show. Named after the eligible prince, Harry is Kennel Club accredited and celebrated his first birthday on 1 April 2015. He likes walking on two legs more than on four. *Britain's Got Talent* beckons … or maybe not.

Downton Abbey

SUNDAY, 9PM

 Upstairs, Downstairs with sturdier sets.

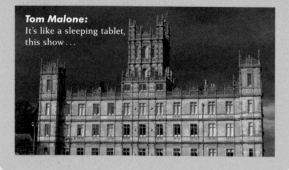

Tom Malone: It's like a sleeping tablet, this show . . .

Downton Abbey Fun Fact

Scarlett is right – the exteriors of *Downton Abbey* are filmed at Highclere Castle in Berkshire, where Peter Andre and Katie Price tied the knot in 2005.

 Amy Tapper: I know it's the olden days, but it's just so dull.

 Baasit Siddiqui: So, when were curtains invented?

 Umar Siddiqui: I imagine they were invented after the window.

 Scarlett Moffatt: That's where Peter Andre and Jordan got married.

 Tom Malone: I'd rather have an episode of piles than watch an episode of that thing.

 Tom Malone Jnr: The good news is: it's ending. The bad news is: you've got to get through another series first.

 Tom Malone: It's like a sleeping tablet, this show.

 Tom Malone Jnr: What do these people do as a job, the posh people?

DOWNTON ABBEY TV BINGO

An emotion being suppressed in the drawing room	A boring conversation about the estate	Someone reading an important global news story in a newspaper at breakfast
Maggie Smith delivering a punchline	Lady Mary knocking back a suitor	A subplot in which someone who can't cook has to pretend to be able to cook and gets Mrs Patmore to secretly do it
The servants lining up to greet a one-off American star in a Christmas special	Anna frowning	Something bad happening in London

Julie Malone: They've got land.

 Tom Malone Jnr: Oh. Land.

 Tom Malone: It's a bit of a girly programme.

 Josh Tapper: I like more action programmes.

 Nikki Tapper: This is lovely.

 Carolyne Michael: Whenever I watch it, I feel like I disappear into another world.

 Chris: What do you want to be when you grow up? I'd like to be someone's skivvy and be called an under-butler.

———— 66 ————

Amy Tapper:

I know it's the olden days, but it's just so dull.

———— 99 ————

 Stephen: I'd like to get under a butler.

 Scarlett Moffatt: You've got buckets of money you wipe your arse on; or you probably get a servant to wipe it.

 Rev. Kate: At least it gives us something to talk to my mum about. She's not overkeen on it, though; it's on ITV. She thinks ITV's a bit common.

Dragons' Den

SUNDAY, 8PM

 Sweating entrepreneurs prostitute inventions and get-rich schemes before four seated, Roman Emperor-like business tycoons who compete to invest or loudly announce that they are 'out', because who needs a sit-on child's suitcase or a reggae-reggae sauce?

 Stephen: The bloke that presents it has one eye going down the shop and the other one coming back for change.

Chris: They're all so sour-faced.

 Stephen: She looks like she's rolling a bogey. Pick, lick, roll, flick. Get out.

 Baasit Siddiqui: Why do they look so serious? They've all got a really mardy look on their face.

 Steph: Forty per cent of f**k-all is still f**k-all.

 Stephen: Invent something that's worth buying.

 Jonathan Tapper: Nonsense programme.

Dragons' Den Fun Fact

The show originated in Japan, where it's called *Mane No Tora*, which means 'Tigers of Money'.

"

Amy Tapper:

Why dragons, why not dinosaurs?

"

GOGGLEBOX TV

Featuring
THE LETTER 'E'

Including
EASTENDERS
EMBARRASSING BODIES

Plus
THE EUROVISION SONG CONTEST

EXCLUSIVE! Eurovision vs. Armageddon!

EastEnders

MONDAY, TUESDAY, THURSDAY, FRIDAY, 7.30PM

BBC1 Second-longest-running BBC soap after the Welsh-language *Pobol y Cwm*. Set in a fictional borough of London's East End, where property is still affordable, and thumbnailed for being 'depressing', because it is. In February 2015, as part of its thirtieth-anniversary celebrations, the BBC broadcast a live episode to answer the question that had been running for nearly a year: who killed Lucy Beale?

Stephen: You can write 'Bobby' at the bottom of it now.

WHO KILLED LUCY BEALE?

Chris: Well, I'm glad that's over.

Stephen: It did drag on. You even got that 'Who killed Lucy Beale?' T-shirt. You can write 'Bobby' at the bottom of it now.

WALFORD
(ENTER AT OWN RISK)

EastEnders Fun Fact

A study in the *BMJ* (*British Medical Journal*) worked out that living in Walford is more dangerous than being a bomb-disposal expert, a Formula One driver or a steeplejack.

I DO DOCUMENTARIES NOW

FAAAAAAAAMILY

Embarrassing Bodies

MONDAY, 9PM

CH4 Privates are often on parade in this BAFTA-winning medical roadshow where members of the public with lumps, folds and rashes too 'embarrassing' to show to their doctor show them to millions of us instead.

 Amy Tapper: *Embarrassing Bodies* is all lumps on your willy and problems with your clits.

 Nikki Tapper: Amy!

 Dom: He's funny. He's got a sense of humour.

 Steph: Well, you'd have to if you were looking at knobs all day.

 Baasit Siddiqui: When do you realize in life that you want to become a penis doctor?

TV Food Tips

Anything but a banana.

The Eurovision Song Contest

First held in 1956, this annual karaoke extravaganza doesn't seem to be going away.

 Tom Malone: At the end of the Second World War they were all killing each other; fifteen years later, they're having a sing-off.

 Giles: In an increasingly wicked and dangerous world it gives us a break from … nuclear Armageddon. (he listens to 'Save All Your Kisses For Me') This is the sort of song that would come into your mind on your deathbed.

Giles:

In an increasingly wicked and dangerous world it gives us a break from ... nuclear Armageddon.

GOGGLEBOX TV

Featuring
THE LETTER 'F'

Including
FIFA WORLD CUP
FIFTY SHADES OF GREY
FILM QUIZ

Plus
FIRST DATES
FOOD

and
FOUR ROOMS

EXCLUSIVE! Watching the 1966 World Cup with the Goggleboxers!

★ THE GOGGLEBOX ★

MAGICAL HISTORY TOUR

Through the power of TV, we take you back to 1966

FIFA World Cup, 30 July 1966

Held in England and the last World Cup to be broadcast in fuzzy black and white, the host nation beat West Germany 4–2 at the Wembley final after extra time, with Geoff Hurst's second goal clouded in controversy. We watch the last few minutes of the match, including a third goal from Hurst, and then commentator Kenneth Wolstenholme's immortal line, 'They think it's all over ...'

Mark Moffatt: It is now!

 Scarlett Moffatt: Is that where that comes from?

 Mark Moffatt: Aye. We were all born in World Cup years: I was '66, Elizabeth's '70, Scarlett's '90 and our Ava's 2006. A strange coincidence.

 Scarlett Moffatt: England will never, ever win again.

Football looked very different then to how it looks now.

 Scarlett Moffatt: Not a headband in sight. No diamond earrings.

No optical-illusion adverts painted on the pitch.

 Scarlett Moffatt: That's why it looks so empty, cos there's no adverts down the side.

 Betty Moffatt: It looks like a game of football. Football is all about wages and sponsors now, and they weren't on the astronomical amounts the players are on these days. It was more like a hobby they were really good at. So you could win the World Cup on the Friday and be back at work on Monday as a postie or a brickie.

 Mark Moffatt: And that linesman – where's he from? Lithuania?

Azerbaijan.

 Mark Moffatt: He's got a statue. He's the most famous person from there.

 Scarlett Moffatt: I don't like the World Cup.

 Lee: Didn't they have colour tellies in them days?

 Jenny: The ball looks real heavy, doesn't it? What a great achievement – and yet look at the money they was on. They was all working at the same time. That's what they should do, bring it all back.

 Rev. Kate: It is now! It always makes me laugh that there was somebody called Nobby.

 Giles: Was this with Eusébio? I would have been aware of it, but we weren't a footy family.

 Mary: What else happened in '66? Everest?

 Giles: No.

 Mary: The Queen's wedding was on the same day as Everest.

"

Tom Malone Jnr:

We're shit aren't we?

"

 Giles: How short their shorts are compared to now. Bobby Moore. I think it was a proud moment, but it didn't feature very highly in our house.

 Julie Malone: I was three. Is that the last time we won it? God. The only time as well?

 Tom Malone Jnr: We're shit, aren't we?

 Julie Malone: Was that George Best?

All men: No!

 Tom Malone Jnr: He was Northern Irish.

Julie Malone: Was that Bobby Charlton with the baldy head?

Nikki Tapper: Is this Charlie George?

 Jonathan Tapper: One of the goals, the third one, didn't actually cross the line.

 Amy Tapper: I've never heard that before: 'They think it's all over, it is now.'

 Leon: We were watching this. It wasn't a goal, it bounced down, so Germany might have won it. But because they were the home nation, England got the best of the decisions. I do think England could one day win [again], but there are too many foreign players over here, so English youngsters don't come through now. It's not gonna change. The England manager is often a yes-man, like Hodgson. The last great manager was Alf Ramsey, I think.

 June: You're a club man, aren't you?

 Leon: I prefer club football.

 June: Didn't Everton win the Cup that year?

 Leon: They did. That's more of a memory for me. I saw them at Wembley. I borrowed the housekeeping money. The ticket was ten shillings. I paid five pounds. June gave it to me.

 June: And you never knew when it might happen again.

 Stephen: This is all they go on about, still, don't they?

 Chris: It's in black and white – you can't even tell who's playing who. They all look the same.

 Stephen: This reminds me of when Dickie Davies used to do it when we were kids.

 Andrew Michael: I was seven years old and had no interest.

 Carolyne Michael: I remember it very well and I knew the names of all the players.

 Andrew Michael: Imagine scoring three goals in a World Cup final. You're a god, basically.

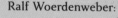

Ralf Woerdenweber:

My question is: what did England win after '66? And what did Germany win?

 Carolyne Michael: I loved Gordon Banks. I thought he was the nicest one.

 Ralf Woerdenweber: Don't start a discussion with me. It wasn't a goal.

 Eve Woerdenweber: That was definitely a goal.

 Ralf Woerdenweber: Not that goal, the header.

 Eve Woerdenweber: It still would have been 3–2.

 Ralf Woerdenweber: It split Germany in two halves, I can tell you that. You didn't have the cameras on the field that you have today. But I was only three. My question is: what did England win after '66? And what did Germany win?

 Viv Woerdenweber: We won the Eurovision Song Contest.

 Sandra: Bobby Moore and George Best are the only two people I know. And they're dead now.

GARY WILL SEE YOU NOW

Fifty Shades of Grey

 In February 2015, the film adaptation of the gajillion-selling erotic novel hit our screens and broke box-office records around the world.

———— " ————

Umar Siddiqui:

I was confused. I thought it was 'Fifty Shades of Gary'.

———— " ————

 Sandra: I used to be a domination man.

 Sandy: Dominatric?

 Sandra: Tek off your trousers. I've got a whip. (whips herself in face) I'm bleeding.

GUESS THE FILM

FILM QUIZ

Test your film knowledge and tell us which films our Goggleboxers are describing.

(Answers opposite. No cheating.)

 1. Rev. Kate: The bus that couldn't slow down.

 2. Rev. Kate: Man fluffs his lines on a train.

 3. Rev. Kate: Neglectful parents employ witch to babysit children.

 4. Graham: Father cross-dresses to win back kids' hearts.

 5. Rev. Kate: Mother is brutally murdered. Father loses son and employs dimwitted accomplice to help him find his son.

 6. Jenny: A singer's coming up for a big award and gets death threats. So she takes her son to a safe house.

 7. Lee: Clickety-click. A girl in red slippers wants to go home.

 8. Scarlett Moffatt: Amazing hair. A bit of bestiality. Lots of singing. Dancing teacups.

 9. Betty Moffatt: Italian. Mafia. Funny like a clown.

 10. Mark Moffatt: Chariots. Gladiators. Lots of sandals. On the cross.

 11. Mary: Young boy running through meadows in the early 1920s or something like that, with a wonderful musical soundtrack, and a story of how different things were in the past.

 12. Tom Malone Jnr: A very unlucky policeman at Christmas.

 13. Josh Tapper: There's this guy and he gets bullied and he can't run – at first.

 14. Amy Tapper: There's two people and they fall in love, and you find out at the end that the whole thing they're telling you is their story, but the woman has dementia.

 15. Josef: A failed attempt to get away on a motorbike.

 16. Josef: An attempt to steal some gold bars which ends in a cliffhanger.

Josef:

An attempt to steal some gold bars which ends in a cliffhanger.

> 66
>
> Amy Tapper:
>
> ***There's two people and they fall in love, and you find out at the end that the whole thing they're telling you is their story, but the woman has dementia.***
>
> 99

17. Bill: Love and war in Morocco.

18. Leon: A love story and a great accident.

19. June: Love, revolution and parting.

20. Andrew Michael: Schizophrenia and maths.

21. Louis Michael: Jungle man.

22. Carolyne Michael: There's a lady in a boat, and there are seven children, and they all get up and stand up at the same time, and they all fall into the water.

23. Carolyne Michael: There's another lake, and another boat, and there's a brother, and he's out in the boat with somebody, and there's just the two of them. And he gets shot.

24. Carolyne Michael: There's a family and it's the early sixties and they go and stay at this big campsite, and they see all the other people arriving and one of the daughters says, 'Oh, I should have brought my coral shoes!' and she's really upset.

25. Viv Woerdenweber: A magical fantasy for grown-ups, and children. An unwanted, orphaned baby with nothing, who goes on to have everything every little boy has dreamed of.

ANSWERS

1. *Speed*
2. *The Great Escape*
3. *Nanny McPhee*
4. *Mrs Doubtfire*
5. *Finding Nemo*
6. *The Bodyguard*
7. *The Wizard of Oz*
8. *Beauty and the Beast*
9. *Goodfellas*
10. *Ben-Hur*
11. *The Go-Between*
12. *Die Hard*
13. *Forrest Gump*
14. *The Notebook*
15. *The Great Escape*
16. *The Italian Job*
17. *Casablanca*
18. *Titanic*
19. *Doctor Zhivago*
20. *A Beautiful Mind*
21. *Tarzan*
22. *The Sound of Music*
23. *The Godfather: Part II*
24. *Dirty Dancing*
25. *Harry Potter and the Philosopher's Stone*

First Dates

WEDNESDAY, 10PM

CH4 Reality show that does what it says on the tin, eavesdropping on maiden romantic dinners, ideally with at least one boorish, overplucked suitor for comedy/cringe value.

Leon: I think it's lovely when a boy meets a girl and they live happily ever after.

 Leon: I'm a great believer in true love. I think it's lovely when a boy meets a girl and they live happily ever after.

 Lee: I couldn't do that, go into a restaurant and be filmed on your first date. Could you?

 Jenny: No.

 Lee: You'd get soup all down your top.

 Jenny: I know.

 Giles: I think people should just have arranged marriages. Like us. Ours was an arranged marriage. You arranged it.

 Mary: I did.

 Tom Malone: Julie chased me for months. They didn't have restraining orders at the time. She got me in the end at some pub in Gorton, wasn't it?

 Julie Malone: Tom's opening line was, 'I knew I should have put me heels on tonight.'

 Tom Malone: She was that much bigger than me.

Food

 Bill: Elvis Presley's only TV commercial was for Southern Maid Donuts in 1954. His sole line of dialogue was: 'You get 'em piping hot after 4am.'

 Tom Malone Jnr: Jam tarts must be one of your five a day because of the jam, the fruit.

 Tom Malone: If you have a fruit biscuit, that's one of your five a day.

 Julie Malone: No, it isn't.

 Tom Malone: An orange Club.

 Leon: Do you want some cold custard?

June: No.

Leon: You're a funny one.

> 66
>
> Tom Malone:
>
> *If you have a fruit biscuit, that's one of your five a day.*
>
> 99

 Sandy: You know you're meant to chew everything forty times.

 Sandra: I ain't got time to count. You mad?

 Bill: Have you noticed how many of the best things in life begin with 'Ch'? Cheese, chocolate, champagne, chess. You can live on those.

 Josef: Cheese with a few grapes.

 Bill: You'd have to have cherries.

Four Rooms

SUNDAY, 7PM

CH4 *Antiques Roadshow* meets *Dragons' Den*: collectibles offered to four dealers who offer way less than expected and the race to the bottom begins.

Stephen: A bit of f**king wood.

 Stephen: So basically, you turn up with a bit of old shit.

 Chris: And go into a room.

 Stephen: These lot come out, check it out. Go back into their rooms. And then you go into each room and see what they offer you.

In an episode in February 2015, one contestant brings a piece of oak said to be from HMS Victory, Lord Admiral Nelson's ship.

 Stephen: A bit of f**king wood.

As all the Goggleboxers point out: how can he prove it actually came from HMS Victory? He claims: *'You can smell Trafalgar.'*

 Tom Malone Jnr: What does Trafalgar smell like?

 Tom Malone: Pigeon shit.

He is asking for £50k.

 Scarlett Moffatt: Who's Nelson? Mandela?

 Betty Moffatt: Nelson Mandela's ship.

 Mark Moffatt: From the 1700s?

Josh Tapper:

When was the Battle of Trafalgar?

Nikki Tapper:

Nineteen sixty…

GOGGLEBOX TV

Featuring
THE LETTER 'G'

Including
GAME OF THRONES
GEORGE CLOONEY
GENERAL ELECTION
GOGGLEBOX

Plus
GRAND NATIONAL
GREAT BRITISH BAKE OFF

EXCLUSIVE! Gogglebox 2015 General Election Special!

Game of Thrones

MONDAY, 9PM

SKY ATLANTIC Impenetrably complex, sort-of-medieval, dynastic fantasy saga involving swords, crowns, armies, coups, battles, torture and gratuitous nudity, now up to five blockbusting seasons.

Dynastic fantasy saga involving swords and boobs.

 Baasit Siddiqui: It's epic. The biggest thing they've done as a TV series. It's like every episode is a mini movie.

 Eve Woerdenweber: Best programme on TV.

 Ralf Woerdenweber: I love it.

 Steph: I'm very excited. My nipples have gone.

 Betty Moffatt: It's like a sexy *Dungeons and Dragons*.

 Giles: There's a lot of sex in it. That's what I've heard from my sixteen-year-old nephew. You'd better look away, Mary. You don't like this sort of thing.

 Josef: We didn't think much of that, did we?

 Bill: Ghastly.

 Josef: If I'd watched it from the beginning, perhaps it would make sense.

 Bill: Apart from the naked breasts, I don't think there was anything in it that I liked.

 Giles: It's like *Carry On Camping* with ponderous music, dim lighting and an absurd storyline.

 Baasit Siddiqui: There's something very attractive about a woman you know full well can kick your arse.

 Sid Siddiqui: No!

 Baasit Siddiqui: OK, that's just me.

 Andrew Michael: Strong female characters can be naked, and it's often good like that.

 Carolyne Michael: Do we get the men, though?

 Chris: If *Game of Thrones* was on Netflix, I would have started watching it. What are there, five series? We just watched the first episode of series five and we're like, 'We don't know any of the characters.' But everyone who's been watching it says it's amazing.

 Stephen: (groans: still not convinced) Hmmmm.

 Chris: I love all that – I love fantasy.

Stephen: Titties.

 Sid Siddiqui: When I said it was similar to *Harry Potter* it was a throwaway remark.

 Baasit Siddiqui: And I said, 'What are you talking about?' Don't get me started on that again!

 Sid Siddiqui: At that point in time, I didn't realize that Baasit was so committed.

> ❝
>
> Giles:
>
> **It's like Carry On Camping with ponderous music, dim lighting and an absurd storyline.**
>
> ❞

GAME OF THRONES TV BINGO

A character you thought was dead who seems to still be alive	A character you thought was still alive who hasn't been seen for an entire season	Gratuitous full-frontal nudity set in a brothel for no narrative reason
The death of a principal character	Someone referring to Jon Snow by his full name	Hodor saying 'Hodor!'
You, recognizing somewhere you went on holiday when it was still called Yugoslavia	Crow!	The entire season's CGI budget blown in one scene

 Baasit Siddiqui: Oh God, yeah, I've read all the books.

 Sid Siddiqui: I realized I'd said something I shouldn't have. I have watched it for a second time and it wasn't as painful.

 Baasit Siddiqui: That's cos there were boobs in it.

———— 66 ————

Andrew Michael:

Strong female characters can be naked, and it's often good like that.

———— 99 ————

George Clooney

 Nikki Tapper: He's so good-looking. He's one of the best-looking men on this Earth. He's stunning.

 Amy Tapper: After Dad.

 Nikki Tapper: Yeah, after Dad.

 Tom Malone Jnr: He's got grey hair.

 Julie Malone: Yeah, but you can still be handsome and distinguished with grey hair.

 Tom Malone: Or no hair.

General Election 2015

This was the most interesting general election ... since the last one. Could Labour under-nerdy Ed Miliband unseat austerity-fixated Conservative toffs, or would 'smaller parties' like UKIP, the Greens and the SNP reshape the 'old politics'? The Ggoggleboxers have been watching it right the way through.

DAVID CAMERON

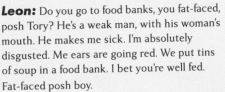

Leon: Do you go to food banks, you fat-faced, posh Tory? He's a weak man, with his woman's mouth. He makes me sick. I'm absolutely disgusted. Me ears are going red. We put tins of soup in a food bank. I bet you're well fed. Fat-faced posh boy.

Scarlett Moffatt: (on Cameron's copy of the letter left by the Labour minister saying, 'There is no money') He wants to get that f**ker laminated!

Giles: If he was any more polished, he'd slip over.

Baasit Siddiqui: He plays up for the cameras. Remember when he was trying to become prime minister, he was seen on his bike everywhere. The second he was prime minister, I haven't seen him on his bike once.

Umar Siddiqui: They should call him David Camera-on.

Amy Tapper: He's got a very big forehead.

Sandy: They've all got a fat head.

NIGEL FARAGE

Leon: He's a dickhead.

Steph: Enoch Powell by another name.

Bill: I think he's one of the most interesting political figures of our time.

June: I can't stand that guy.

Leon: I'd kick *you* out, mate.

 June: His problem is he thinks with his mouth.

 Leon: That's what you say about me.

 Sandy: They talk about people coming into this country. Do you know the percentage of English people that have left this country and gone abroad to other people's countries to live?

 Leon: My father was the son of an immigrant. Is that alright with Nigel Farage?

 Baasit Siddiqui: I don't know what it is but I just can't take him seriously. I don't know if it's his policies or his face.

 Sandy: The rich are getting richer and the poor are getting poorer.

 Giles: I haven't got the trickle-down effect that they say everyone else has got. I still shop at Lidl.

———— " ————

Sandra:

David Cameron is Batman.
Ed Miliband is Robin.
Nigel Farage is the Joker.

———— " ————

> "

Scarlett Moffatt:

I'm not taking political advice from a flipping Hobbit.

"

THE LABOUR PARTY POLITICAL BROADCAST

The Labour Party decided they would use the actor Martin Freeman to try to get their message across.

 Steph: Now, I like Martin Freeman. I think he's fabulous . . .

 Dom: What's that got to do with anything?

 Steph: He's the guy that's just done that.

 Dom: That's not Martin Freeman.

 Steph: Yes, it is.

 Dom: It's not. Martin Freeman is the black guy from . . . Oh, that's Morgan Freeman.

NICK CLEGG

 Leon: He's a bright boy but he sold his soul.

 Baasit Siddiqui: Is that Nick Clegg or an actor playing Nick Clegg? He has the air of a man about to clear his desk.

At one point during the campaigning Clegg seems to be spending most of his time in a car park.

 Rev. Kate: I love it: all the other leaders are out talking to people, meeting with families – and Nick Clegg's in a soggy car park.

 Graham: I think I've been to that car park.

 Rev. Kate: Poor Nick. Five years ago, everyone was on his side. Now there's no one behind him. Literally.

 Steph: I feel sorry for him. I want to make him a hot chocolate and caress his head.

 Dom: And put him to bed. Poor little fella.

One phrase kept coming up repeatedly in the election-night coverage – the idea that a Conservative–Lib Dem coalition would require David Cameron to go into a dark room with Nick Clegg.

 Steph: He looks like he's got bad breath.

 Sandy: He's a trier.

 Sandra: He's a dickhead trier.

 Carolyne Michael: He's a dead man walking.

ED MILIBAND

 Steph: If you look at half his face, the top half's quite nice. The bottom half: absolutely disastrous.

 Chris: He doesn't look like he could run a mile, never mind the country.

At one point, someone on Ed's campaign thought it would be a good idea to put a load of election promises on a massive bit of stone; unsurprisingly, this was soon nicknamed his 'Ed Stone'.

 Giles: He's made so many mistakes. No one will remember this one.

 Scarlett Moffatt: He just comes across as a very nervous person. He never looks people in the eye.

 Rev. Kate: A lot of people look at Ed Miliband and they say he's not very confident and they're taking the mickey out of him because he's not very polished and he's a geek. I quite like that he's not as polished [as the rest of them].

 Giles: He reminds me of a student, who hasn't had any hands-on experience.

 Baasit Siddiqui: He looks like he's on an apprenticeship.

 Chris: Snog Miliband; marry Cameron; and avoid that weasel Nick Clegg. Or we could just tag-team them all?

 Scarlett Moffatt: He's talking about the divide between rich and poor. He's got two kitchens.

 Steph: Did you see, the other kitchen was the nanny's kitchen. Elitist, *moi*?

"

Dom (on Ed Miliband):

How can you trust a man who has two kitchens?

"

 Dom: How can you trust a man who has two kitchens?

 Steph: (looks at Dom)

 Dom: I know we've got five. You can trust a man with five kitchens, but not two.

 Steph: Either one, or five. Nothing in between.

 Giles: He will get the sympathy vote, because the British people love an underdog. He's the Tim Henman of politics.

BORIS JOHNSON

 Leon: He's a buffoon.

 Steph: I think he hides behind his humour so that if it fails he can say, 'Well, it was all a bloody joke anyway.'

Sid Siddiqui: Surely no one in the country could ever imagine him as prime minister?

 Ralf Woerdenweber: I think when he will be the government of England, England will go up.

 Viv Woerdenweber: I think England would be the laughing stock.

 Stephen: Well, I'd vote for him, for definite. Just so we'd get to see more of him and his family. They're hysterical to look at.

 Jonathan Tapper: If you want to like a politician, he'd be the first one.

 Eve Woerdenweber: He's a nutter but he's an amazing nutter.

 Carolyne Michael: You have to beware the fool, because in all Shakespeare's plays he's the clever one.

THERESA MAY

 Stephen: I like Theresa May, but if you saw her in the street, you'd ask her if she needed help getting across the road. 'You alright, love?'

NICOLA STURGEON

 Tom Malone: Whenever I see her, I think of Rab C. Nesbitt's wife.

 Sandra: She moves like a chicken.

 Stephen: She's got an aggressive little stance.

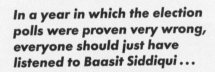

Sandra (on Nicola Sturgeon):

She moves like a chicken.

In a year in which the election polls were proven very wrong, everyone should just have listened to Baasit Siddiqui . . .

 Baasit Siddiqui: I think it'll be the classic thing: stick with the devil you know.

As the sun sets on another round of modern-day electioneering, Stephen reminisces about politics of old . . .

 Stephen: It's not like the scandals in the old days, though, where they used to be caught in stockings and suspenders with an orange in their mouth.

While another Goggleboxer has a vision of the future . . .

 Giles: If I was prime minister, I would give every family in the land a mum's-night-off KFC chicken bucket.

Gogglebox

FRIDAY, 9PM

CH4 Soaraway success that reshaped 'old reality' by filming ordinary people in fixed shots in their living rooms countrywide, watching TV and commenting on it, while never meeting each other, thus maintaining purity of vision; in 2015, a tie-in book hit the bookshops and you are reading it.

ON BEING ASKED TO TAKE PART...

 Giles: Because I use long words on *Gogglebox*, I think I should be paid extra for the Latin roots and derivations...We got on to the programme through a friend of a friend.

 Mary: The *Gogglebox* technique is that they sit in towns and high streets waiting for likely groups of related people to walk by.

 Giles: They said it was quite a relief not to have a white wall and a sofa for a change. There's nothing wrong with that combination, but they quite liked the idea of Laura Ashley ...no, what is this pattern?

 Mary: William Morris.

 Giles: It's called Willow Boughs by William Morris and you get it from Sanderson. The pattern is on the walls and the curtains.

 Mary: I don't particularly like having to watch *Britain's Got Talent*.

 Giles: We struggled with *Comic Relief*, didn't we? I'm not very good on emotional things, because I went to a minor public school and had it knocked out of me. So I'm very good at being flippant at wildlife programmes, but put me in front of something about schizophrenics jumping off bridges and I'm pretty hopeless. Mary gushes a lot.

 Mary: I'm Irish, you see. Mawkish.

 Rev. Kate: If we were sitting on the sofa, I'd sit next to the dog, because he's my dog. After three series of *Gogglebox*, the minute the cameras come in, Buster jumps on the sofa. He hits his mark every time. You're such a pro, Buster!

 Scarlett Moffatt: I get asked to do a lot of stuff, but I like *Gogglebox*. There's no other show like it. I got some tweets today, saying, 'Now that the series is over you'll be doing *Big Brother*.' But I would literally rather pour wasabi sauce in me eyes. They say, 'Does that mean you haven't been asked?' But I have. They sent flowers and everything to try and persuade us, but I think *Gogglebox* is like theatre, whereas *Big Brother*'s like panto. There's nothing else really like it on TV.

Mark Moffatt: We are edited in a good light. No one's edited in a bad light.

Betty Moffatt: But that's a lot to do with the people who are in it. Maybe it's not just editing. Maybe that's just how the people are.

Scarlett Moffatt: Yeah, but sometimes you know how we have arguments, and they don't show them? People don't wanna watch that.

Betty Moffatt: But families do fall out and argue in real life. People do say, 'I've had enough, I'm going to bed.'

Scarlett Moffatt: There was that time when we were arguing about the bedroom tax. I went, 'Right, that's it, I'm off to bed.'

Betty Moffatt: The bedroom tax doesn't even apply to us!

Julie Malone: When they asked us, I said, 'No, I've got five dogs.'

GOGGLEBOX HAS BROUGHT US CLOSER

Tom Malone: I didn't fancy it at all. I'd never seen it. I thought there'd be a camera on all the time. I said to Julie, 'What if I come down in the middle of the night in me underpants? I'm not having that!'

Tom Malone Jnr: As Shaun and I got older, we started doing less watching telly as a group, but *Gogglebox* has made us do it more. It's nice.

Tom Malone: Certain films and programmes, we'd sit down and watch together, but a lot of the time Shaun'll be watching football upstairs, while Julie's watching the soaps.

Shaun Malone: When *Big Bang Theory* comes on, we'll all come down and watch it. And *The Chase*.

Tom Malone: You always like to get together to watch *Elf*, don't you?

Jonathan Tapper: The beauty of *Gogglebox* is that, even though we have the odd argument, it forces us to sit down together and talk, and watch things. Otherwise they'd disappear upstairs.

Amy Tapper: Thank God for *Gogglebox*. It's the only time we all sit down. Normally, Dad's working, or here asleep on the sofa, I'm up in my room doing homework on Pythagoras' theory, Mum's cleaning or probably on the phone, and Josh will be the only one sitting watching politics or Victoria Derbyshire.

Josef: I used to see Bill two, three times a year, maybe. At most. Once a year at the MSO – the Mind Sports Olympiad, that is – and if there's an event I'm taking part in that he's covering, we'd meet there. In the last two or three years, we've met more times than we had in the previous fifteen. We don't hate each other yet, do we?

Bill: No! I think we've got to know each other better. It's been very good.

Josef: He still thinks I'm a philistine because of my attitude to opera, but there we are.

WHEN NEW FAMILIES JOIN . . .

Stephen: Joe Public don't like it when the newbies come in, but I love it. We're a bit loud, Sandy and Sandra are loud, but in the *London Evening Standard* the Siddiquis were voted the best, followed by Jenny and Lee, then the Moffatts. If ever we have a drink and we're playing up, it never makes the edit, does it? We f**k about a lot. When I nearly drowned in a glass of water, you were playing on your phone. He always looks like he's not listening to me when I talk, and he leaves it for a minute, then goes, 'What?' There was one bit where he was eating a brioche, which is quite soft, and I could hear, *crunch, crunch, crunch*. He hadn't noticed, and I went to him, 'Are you eating your f**kin' teeth?'

> 66
>
> Giles:
>
> ## *Because I use long words on Gogglebox, I think I should be paid extra for the Latin roots and derivations . . .*
>
> 99

 Chris: I was having my caps redone, and I had temporaries on, and literally one of them had come off and I was munching it. When he said that, it registered: 'Why's it got a hard bit in it?'

 Stephen: You can't f**kin' script that. But it didn't make it on.

 Carolyne Michael: I think it was Jim Carrey who said something like, the way you make people feel is the greatest currency you have. And I think, for me, that's why I love to do *Gogglebox*, because it makes people happy and spreads the love, and spreads the joy. We're so proud of that. You can't put a price on something like that. It's a privilege.

 Alex Michael: I like it because it breaks up a boring week at work.

 Carolyne Michael: We are ordinary people.

 Andrew Michael: You speak for yourself!

 Carolyne Michael: You're extraordinary.

 Andrew Michael: I get propositioned. Some women don't even ask for a selfie: I literally just get grabbed. It's happened about three times. The reason I do *Gogglebox* is that a happy wife is a happy life.

 Baasit Siddiqui: We watch it separately. For the first series, we weren't particularly fussed, it was a bit nerve-wracking. (to Umar) You still don't watch it.

 Umar Siddiqui: No, I can't bring myself to sit down and watch it. We watch TV in front of the camera, but as far as I'm concerned, that's the end of it!

GOGGLEBOX TV BINGO

Giles using Mary's name	One of the Woerdenweber cats moving	Andrew Michael raising his voice
Sandy calling Sandra 'babes'	Leon praising Amanda Holden's arms	Amy Tapper hiding behind a cushion
A Malone dog licking Tom's face	Betty looking adoringly at Scarlett after a witticism	Lee glaring at Jenny after a daft remark

Sid Siddiqui: To some extent, I'm similar to Umar, but my biggest problem has been that if we've done a good piece, and it's not been shown – for very practical reasons, I'm not blaming anybody – you feel slightly as if you've been cheated after seven or eight hours' filming. That sometimes had a very negative emotional effect on me: 'Why am I watching this? I shouldn't be doing this!' But then one day I did watch it, and I thoroughly enjoyed it. I took advice from Baasit – he said, 'Don't take it personally. We probably weren't good enough, or we weren't suitable, whatever.' And I thought, yes, he's right. I just enjoyed the other people on it. One day my wife said to me, 'Are we watching it?' and I said, 'No, no, I don't like it,' and she said, 'Well, I like it. If you don't want to watch it, don't.' It's similar to if you have a meal, and make a special effort to sit together and eat together. It forces you to get together. It has a tremendous pull, and the whole nation seems to be pulled together.

 Baasit Siddiqui: Social media really helps. We're not the loud ones that say loads and loads of stuff and make rude gestures. It's usually short, sharp reactions. But what we do say is tweeted and quoted.

WHY IT COULD NEVER BE SCRIPTED

 Eve Woerdenweber: What you see is what we're like. Ralf swears, I swear, Mum swears, the cats are happy.

 Ralf Woerdenweber: If we did one show of *Gogglebox* scripted, people would say, 'This is not Ralf, this is not Eve, this is not June, this is not Leon.'

Gogglebox Fun Fact

The two pieces of music used are the songs 'Perfect World' and 'Brand New Day' by the Irish band Kodaline.

Grand National

Britain's most iconic horse race, held annually at Aintree Racecourse in Liverpool.

 Sid Siddiqui: It's an event, isn't it? A special day of the year.

 Baasit Siddiqui: I get knackered watching it. It beats the Lottery though, doesn't it.

 Sandy: I love it every year. This is celebration time. Everybody's in the bookies, you know.

Great British Bake Off

'Soggy bottoms'

WEDNESDAY, 8PM

BBC1 The competitive cookery show that reshaped competitive cookery by staging it in a marquee in the grounds of a *Downton*-style house and giving bakers hours to bake a cake/pie/bun/Alaska/eclair while presenters Mel and Sue lick their forks; more than a show, a way of life.

Steph: It makes me hungry, watching this. But it doesn't make me want to bake, if I'm honest. Some other f**ker can do it.

GREAT BRITISH BAKE OFF TV BINGO

'Soggy bottom'	'Nice crumb'	A baker being praised by the judges for at least making the right number of scones even though they're inedible
A baker kneeling beside an oven as if in prayer	'You've obviously had a few problems'	A blue plaster!
Mel and/or Sue making a sexual innuendo that would make Alan Carr blush	A lone employee of the country house in a green Barbour jacket walking past the tent in the background	A shot of rain-lashed bunting flapping in the wind

GOGGLEBOX TV

Featuring
THE LETTER 'H'

Including
HITLER
HOME ALONE
HOMELAND

Plus
HUNTERS OF THE SOUTH SEAS

EXCLUSIVE! Watching Hunters of the South Seas with the Siddiquis!

Hitler, Adolf

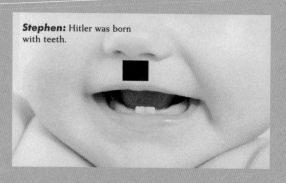

Stephen: Hitler was born with teeth.

Stephen: Hitler was born with teeth.

Chris: The dirty evil bastard.

> 66

Ralf Woerdenweber:

Can we get this straight, please? He's Austrian.

> 99

Home Alone

12A Slapstick comedy from 1990 in which child star Macaulay Culkin must fend for himself when abandoned by mistake in the lavish family home and repel two burglars using Road Runner-style cunning.

Carolyne Michael: That's what you want at Christmas: you want to feel good, all warm and fuzzy inside.

Ralf Woerdenweber: My parents forgot me on the motorway in a car park. Everyone was in the car, I was still in the loo. I stayed there crying my eyes out. Fookin' hell.

Steph: (imagining Culkin's character's reaction as his parents return home at the end of the film) Where the f**k have you been?!

Dom: What do you mean, 'Happy Christmas'? I haven't eaten for three days.

Viv Woerdenweber: You don't hear of him now, do you?

Carolyne Michael: They always have a nice feel-good factor, don't they, these films? That's what you want at Christmas: you want to feel good, all warm and fuzzy inside.

> 66

Steph:

Thank God that's over. Can we watch some porn now?

> 99

Homeland

SUNDAY, 9PM

CH4 Initially compelling post-9/11 counter-terrorism drama from the US, starring Etonian Damian Lewis as a Marine 'turned' by al-Qaeda, whose nemesis is a bipolar female CIA agent. Chris and Stephen found it compelling for all sorts of reasons.

Chris:
We all like a bad boy, don't we?

Stephen:
*Yeah, but not a f**king terrorist.*

 Chris: We all like a bad boy, don't we?

 Stephen: Yeah, but not a f**king terrorist. There's a bad boy and then there's evil. Would you like Hitler?

 Stephen: I wanna know the mindset for someone who goes, 'I'm brainwashed. I think it's a good idea. I'm gonna strap a bomb to myself and blow myself up.'

 Chris: Because I'm gonna get rewarded in the next life.

 Stephen: Seven virgins you get.

 Chris: Why would you wanna go with seven virgins?

 Stephen: You'd want seven dirty old things, wouldn't you?

 Chris: Being a spy. I'd like the acting, pretending to be someone you're not.

 Stephen: Could you try it now?

Watching

HUNTERS OF THE SOUTH SEAS

with THE SIDDIQUIS

 This proves to be the second-hardest *Gogglebox* house to which to gain entry, as there's a shared entrance, rapping upon which fails to alert a soul to my perfectly timed presence. I'm left standing outside like a spare part at a wedding. Literally: a couple have just got married at the church up the road, and guests are returning to their cars as I hover self-consciously by the most famous numbered wheelie bins in Britain, hoping for the best. Eventually, Umar, 37, whose house this is, and who always looks slightly surprised, opens the door,

apologizing for the confusion. (I'd been ringing the wrong bell, which, luckily, doesn't work.)

> 66
>
> Sid Siddiqui:
>
> ## *I can make a decent biryani with my eyes closed.*
>
> 99

He makes me a coffee, offers biscuits and proudly shows me the pieces of coloured tape on his front room's laminate wood floor: left by the *Gogglebox* crew to indicate where to position their cameras. His dad Sid, 70, and younger brother Baasit, 33, tap at the front window to announce their arrival outside. So that's the protocol! The end-of-series hamper is unsealed and posher biscuits and yogurt-covered raisins are shared out.

'We're recluses, aren't we?' says Sid, an NHS manager. 'We keep ourselves to ourselves,' adds Baasit, the teacher, more heavily bearded than we're used to seeing him. I note that, of the trio, only scientist Umar is wearing socks under the Siddiqui house uniform of sailing pumps. Sid looks pretty cool, sockless.

Their surname means 'truthful' in Arabic, and an unforced air of honesty follows them around. They are easy company, as if you've known them all your life. 'We occupy this kind of middle ground,' reasons Umar. 'And for some people to see a Muslim family that aren't too extreme, that's a breath of fresh air, isn't it?'

'Do you want to hold the blue tits?' asks Umar as we arrange ourselves on the maroon leather *Gogglebox* sofa for a selfie, referring to the ornithological ceramic ornament that's been a domestic touchstone since day one. Umar, who keeps a copy of *1001 Movies You Must See Before You Die* in the smallest room, confesses to not being able to bring himself to watch the show, but it's as much out of professionalism as coyness: 'If I see myself act in a certain way that I don't like, it might discourage me from acting like that [in the future].' They're self-aware enough to know that they are, in Umar's shorthand, 'the Soundbite Family'. Sid's wife, the boys'

mother, enjoys watching it, however, and forced Sid to get over himself and do the same.

Baasit is currently struggling with a reputation he has unwittingly cultivated at his local Asda. He's known there as 'Chicken Guy'. Why? 'I think it's because they look into my basket and all I've got is chicken,' he explains, fiddling with his mug with a rabbit on it. His notoriety recently came to a head. 'The other day I went in for half a garlic chicken and there were no halves left, and you could sense the woman's irritation when she had to cut one in half,' he relates, with the utmost gravity, recalling with some embarrassment the world-weariness with which the assistant said, 'I'll go and get the scissors.' He's seriously considering changing supermarkets, and Umar encourages him, saying, 'It's not the same as being known as "Swordfish Guy".'

This reminds Sid to pick up some fish pakoras from a favoured local Asian market on the way home. He's a capable, self-taught cook, by all accounts. 'I can make a decent biryani with my eyes closed,' he confirms.

'As long as it's got chicken in, I'm happy,' says Chicken Guy.

> Baasit Siddiqui:
>
> *As long as it's got chicken in it, I'm happy.*

Hunters of the South Seas

SUNDAY, 9PM

BBC2 South Asia-enamoured writer and explorer Will Millard communes with the extraordinary subsistence fisherfolk of the Coral Triangle in the Western Pacific, all of whom can swim really well. BBC2 offers a warning which skirts around actually saying, 'Warning: Contains whale hunting.'

Baasit Siddiqui: Moby-Dick was a sperm whale.

I budge up next to Sid, feeling overdressed in my socks, and sink into the generous maw of the leather sofa, momentarily feeling part of Britain's most relaxing family as we watch these South Seas-based hunters live a slightly more fraught and salty life.

Umar Siddiqui: It's like *Waterworld* with Kevin Costner.

Sid Siddiqui: It's great that we're going there to explore, but you feel like you're spoiling it for them. Just by being there.

Umar Siddiqui: Are whales endangered?

Sid Siddiqui: For these guys living on this remote coral, there's nothing else there, so their survival depends on fishing. If they're hunting whales, I think that's justifiable. And the hunting they do is not mechanized.

On the screen, Will admits he is 'uneasy' about being there. 'Like most people in the West, the slaughter of whales is difficult to contemplate.'

Sid Siddiqui: So at this moment in time, his opinion is that they shouldn't be doing it?

Baasit Siddiqui: You'd think if they were eating whales, they'd look a bit bigger.

Umar Siddiqui: You can't eat blubber, can you?

Baasit Siddiqui: Is that the equivalent of gristle? Or bacon rind? Mind you, I'm a bit stubborn, I will try and eat as much gristle as I can.

Sid Siddiqui: They're not that remote if they've got all these mod cons. It seems like reasonable accommodation. They've got plenty of plastic bottles.

Umar Siddiqui: They've probably got Starbucks.

Sid Siddiqui: What did he put in his mouth? Is that whale meat?

Baasit Siddiqui: There's nothing worse than eating old whale.

Umar Siddiqui: People are really against eating whale, aren't they? They'd rather eat a Welsh person than eat whales. Is it because they're intelligent? Oh no, that's dolphins.

Sid Siddiqui: There's plentiful meat there. You make one kill and it lasts you six months. And they use the oil for lamps.

Baasit Siddiqui: Is that a Nottingham Forest T-shirt?

Umar Siddiqui: Liverpool. Do you think he's a Liverpool fan?

Baasit Siddiqui: How are they going to catch whales in these crappy boats?

Umar Siddiqui: You're right. If you were going to go out to hunt the largest animal on Earth, you'd want a better boat, wouldn't you? More like a warship.

Baasit Siddiqui: Moby-Dick was a sperm whale. I am intrigued to see how they're gonna do this.

An intrepid South Sea hunter literally hurls himself off the boat, with his spear, into the water at a whale.

Umar Siddiqui: Missed it! How do you miss something that big? It's like using a toothpick to catch a monkey.

Baasit Siddiqui: It's less cowardly than shooting a harpoon at it.

Umar Siddiqui: He was really determined. He looks about ninety years old as well.

Baasit Siddiqui: He's just standing on this boat. I struggle on a train.

Sid Siddiqui: He's been doing it forty years, Baasit.

Umar Siddiqui: It's going to be really hard to get the whale back to shore, if they do catch one.

They downscale to chasing a manta ray rather than Moby-Dick; it's that or row home empty-handed. Six hours at sea has yielded just a single fish.

Sid Siddiqui: It's only small, though.

Umar Siddiqui: And they divvy it up among the people that were involved in catching it.

Baasit Siddiqui:

All fish tastes the same. Can you tell the difference between cod and haddock when you get it from the chip shop?

Baasit Siddiqui: It's a nice bit of fish, though. What does Will get? Is anyone else getting hungry watching this?

Sid Siddiqui: If it was chicken, it would be just enough for you.

Umar Siddiqui: Do you think there'll ever be a documentary where they're hunting chicken and we all feel bad about it?

Baasit Siddiqui: You could, like, breed fish, surely? Have, like, a little pond.

Umar Siddiqui: All fish, even John West tuna, is all from fishing, isn't it?

Sid Siddiqui: There are fish farms.

Baasit Siddiqui: That's what they need to be doing.

Sid Siddiqui: I wonder what manta would taste like?

Baasit Siddiqui: All fish tastes the same. Can you tell the difference between cod and haddock when you get it from the chip shop?

Sid Siddiqui: It's a slightly different texture.

Baasit Siddiqui: We're not a fish family, are we? Dad, you used to take us swimming, didn't you?

Umar Siddiqui: At junior school.

Sid Siddiqui: I learned to swim in a river when I was eight, just on my own.

Umar Siddiqui: No supervision?

Baasit Siddiqui: No floats?

Sid Siddiqui: No.

Baasit Siddiqui: Speedos?

Sid Siddiqui: I have caught a fish just by dangling a hook on a piece of string in the water, with a lugworm on the end. Just like that. Dead easy.

Baasit Siddiqui: That manta's not as big as yesterday's manta.

Sid Siddiqui: But if they're not catching enough, they're not surviving, and there's no population explosion. It's natural selection.

Umar Siddiqui: Here, you get a panic if Sainsbury's is closing.

Baasit Siddiqui: Oh God, it's a Sunday, it's closing at four!

Talking of which, thanks to the good work of some missionaries a couple of centuries ago, the predominantly Christian tribe isn't allowed to hunt on a Sunday, even though they're starving and sperm whales are visible at sea.

Baasit Siddiqui: You can imagine the whales mooning at them.

The next day, the water's too rough for them to take out the boats.

Baasit Siddiqui: They just can't catch a break. Still, at least it's always sunny there.

Thankfully – or not – they do harpoon a sperm whale before the episode is out, but not without some maritime confusion and a couple of spear-misses. It's edge-of-the-boat stuff.

Baasit Siddiqui: Look at all that blood.

Sid Siddiqui: It's carnage. Will's having a nervous breakdown. Why did he volunteer to go there?

Baasit Siddiqui: You'd think you'd mind less the bigger it is, because it can defend itself. But these people don't live unless they catch this.

Sid Siddiqui: It's the same old story. I wouldn't want to see a chicken being killed in front of me before I eat it.

Baasit Siddiqui: Unless that chicken had pecked you earlier.

———— 66 ————

Umar Siddiqui:

Here, you get a panic if Sainsbury's is closing.

———— 99 ————

GOGGLEBOX TV

Featuring
THE LETTER "I"

Including
I'M A CELEBRITY... GET ME OUT OF HERE!

INDIANA JONES AND THE TEMPLE OF DOOM

And
THE ISLAND WITH BEAR GRYLLS

EXCLUSIVE! Watching The Island with Bear Grylls with Stephen & Chris!

I'm a Celebrity… Get Me Out of Here!

WEEKDAYS, 9PM

ITV Durable jungle-based endurance test for washed-up VIPs, subject to audience vote and ability to eat disgusting things or be showered with disgusting things in exchange for toilet paper, presented by Ant and Dec on a walkway.

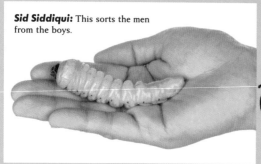

Sid Siddiqui: This sorts the men from the boys.

 Leon: I love 'Get Me Out of the Jungle'.

 The Michael family: (in unison with each other and Ant and Dec onscreen) Get me out of here!

 Carolyne Michael: That's the best bit.

 Stephen: I wonder if they get bored of shouting, 'Get me out of here!' They do it every episode, every series.

 Sid Siddiqui: This sorts the men from the boys.

 Chris: If you were doing the challenge, you'd want to do the best you can.

 Stephen: I wouldn't. I'd get one star and think, that's my dinner sorted. F**k the others.

 Leon: I could present this better than them.

 June: You sit in that chair and you could do everything. Why don't you go and do it?

 Leon: Nobody's asked me to do it. I'd like to go on it to punch them both.

———— 66 ————

Sandra
(on Edwina Currie, referencing her affair with John Major):

If she can take that willy, she can take the jungle.

———— 99 ————

Sid Siddiqui: I don't think you could last a day.

 Baasit Siddiqui: I could last two days.

 Scarlett Moffatt: I could last a year. I've been to worse holiday camps.

 Dom: Why, in all of this, have we not come up with kangaroo vaginas, ever? Why haven't we got a crocodile vagina? (he imagines the challenge) 'We've got forty-five crocodile vaginas, in this bowl, that you've got to stick your tongue in, pick it up with your tongue and drop it into the other bowl.' I've got to write to these guys, in this filthy jungle.

 Tom Malone: Every year they put in celebrities who only old people know.

 Sandra: (on Edwina Currie, referencing her affair with John Major) If she can take *that* willy, she can take the jungle.

 Baasit Siddiqui: That's why I like this: it's only three weeks of your life wasted.

I'M A CELEBRITY… TV BINGO

A celebrity refusing to get into the helicopter	Testicles!	'There's a snake in the camp!'
Someone crying in the diary room because it's hard	Gratuitous bikini shot for the tabloids	A celebrity being strapped into a harness
A romance blossoming	Ant and Dec making the camera crew laugh	Coffin!

Indiana Jones and the Temple of Doom

12A Prequel to *Raiders of the Lost Ark* in which Harrison Ford's alpha antiquarian battles Indian cultists to acquire mystical stone, giving it the full big-budget Saturday-morning-cinema cliffhanger.

Tom Malone Jnr: He's just a professor who finds himself in the middle of it.

Shaun Malone: He's like Bruce Willis in *Die Hard*: he's proper unlucky, isn't he? The first one's the best one.

Tom Malone Jnr: Severus Snape's in it.

Stephen: Why can't you look like him?

Chris: Why can't *you* look like him?

Stephen: I do a little bit.

Rev. Kate: Well, hello Harrison.

Giles: And this is why we don't want our daughter to go on a gap year. She'll go across a rope bridge, because all her friends say it's safe. And then crocodiles will eat her.

Viv Woerdenweber: I like it when he gets his whip out.

Leon: It's a boy's film, this.

June: Sexist.

Julie Malone: He's stupid.

Shaun Malone: *Indiana Jones* isn't stupid.

Julie Malone: Yes he is.

Tom Malone Jnr: He's not stupid, it's got a bit of history to it. You learn stuff watching *Indiana Jones*.

Tom Malone: Don't mess with snakes.

Julie Malone: I still don't like it.

Watching
THE ISLAND WITH BEAR GRYLLS
with STEPHEN AND CHRIS

As I ring the doorbell of Chris's bungalow in sun-kissed Hove, Stephen pulls up behind me onto the drive in his car. Not knowing which way to turn, I wave to Stephen just as Chris opens the door, and I hear myself saying, 'You're coming at me from both directions.' It's a perfect entrance. Everything's an innuendo with the tattooed hairdressers.

It's a baking-hot day on the south coast, although I suspect Chris, 39, would be in short shorts even if there was a foot of snow on the ground. Gloriously bronzed, he invites me in and

introduces me to an unexpected, yet-to-be-televised dog, Fred the basset hound.

> " ———
>
> Stephen:
>
> ***I can't turn off me bleedin' warning lights!***
>
> ——— "

I'm left in the hall while Chris goes out to attend to Stephen, 44, who seems reluctant or unable to step out of the vehicle. 'I can't turn off me bleedin' warning lights!' he shouts in that post-war East End accent. While a crisis is averted (I think a manly neighbour intervened), I reassure the doleful-looking dog in his chic red collar. It's a typically melodramatic start to an afternoon of belly laughs in what might be the best-kept house on *Gogglebox*. Stephen, who likes 'anything housey or gardeny' on TV, shows off the recently curved edges of the back lawn.

The coffees come out in mugs instantly recognizable from three years' loyal service on *Gogglebox* – Stephen gets 'Grumpy Old Man', I feel privileged to receive 'Drama Queen!' and Chris sups from a personalized 'It's All Gone Tits Up' – and a tin of posh cherry shortbreads is liberated from an end-of-series *Gogglebox* gift hamper. Stephen turns his attention to the new household pet. 'He needs a bloody bath,' he sniffs, motioning to the dog. 'He'll make your house smell. He's pungent.' Chris protests that he can't even lift him, but promises to send him to the groomer's once a week when he's a permanent resident.

The ex-couple couldn't be more comfortable around each other, and nothing is off limits. Many of their anecdotes are X-rated, with strong language from the start, told with indiscreet abandon and naming names at every turn. But what's said in Chris's bungalow *stays* in Chris's bungalow. At one point, Stephen remarks to his sparring partner, 'You've got some filthy friends.' I frequently find myself saying, 'Well, *that* won't be in the book,' to which Chris will reply, 'Why not? You can put it in.' They enjoy the fame *Gogglebox* has brought them – they met 'Ian Beale' at the Broadcasting Guild Press Awards 2014 – but are still bemused when parents present them with their ten-year-old daughters, saying, 'She loves you on the show!' Stephen gurns. 'I'm like, really?'

My request to see Ginge in the flesh, or fur, results in Chris leaping from the sofa to call the cat's name around the house. 'Rattle the food box,' offers Stephen. Once the noble old marmalade cat is brought before me for a snapshot, Stephen demands that Chris cleans the sleep out of Ginge's eyes. 'I can't do that,' protests Chris squeamishly. 'Why not?' Stephen retorts impatiently. 'You're his mummy!' In the end, he attends to the task himself.

When it's time to watch TV, Ginge slopes back into the bowels of the bungalow

and Fred snoozes aromatically as I nestle in next to Chris's exposed knees. After a bit of debate, we settle on The Island with Bear Grylls.

The Island with Bear Grylls

WEDNESDAY, 9PM

CH4 Two teams of paintballing types are voluntarily marooned on Pacific atolls and forced to kill a supplied pig to survive, while Bear Grylls records some links.

Chris: They probably fly him out to the island to do a couple of links, then fly him back to his five-star hotel.

In the episode we watch, we join the men's team when they have been on the island for fifteen days, surviving on a 'meagre diet' of coconut and limpets.

Chris: They're ruthless, the women. The men all just sit around going *boo-hoo-hoo-hoo*, while the women are out there killing everything! Anything that's alive on the island. We met a couple of the guys from the last series, didn't we? One of them, oh, he was so dishy. The black guy. He was beautiful.

Stephen: It's not like *I'm a Celebrity…Get Me Out of Here!*, is it? This is proper. I wouldn't do this if they gave me all the tea in China.

Chris: That, to me, is a nightmare. Most people, when they get hungry, get grouchy. Can you imagine what it must be like on that island? Awful.

Stephen: You'd be alright, Chris, you could offer everyone a bit of entertainment.

Chris: I'd say, 'Look, what is the one thing that takes your mind off food?' Sex. If there's one thing men are thinking about, it's sex. OK? So I would be there to offer them sex. I don't want to say what kind of diet I'd be on.

Bear Grylls sums things up from the comfort of his schooner.

Stephen: Bear looks awful, he looks really rough.

Chris: He's looking particularly old, I think.

Stephen: Well, so would you if you'd f**kin' spent a lifetime doing that, chasing pigs.

Chris: They probably fly him out to the island to do a couple of links, then fly him back to his five-star hotel. If you go to a place like that, all you're thinking about is topping up your tan. You don't want to be thinking, oh my God, I've got to go and find food.

Stephen: Their eyes look a bit sunken, like heroin addicts.

Chris: It's like when Matthew McConaughey lost weight for *Dallas Buyers Club*. He looked awful. But since he did that movie I don't think he's looked as good as he looked before. He looks a bit drawn.

Stephen and Chris take a liking to one of the islanders, the seemingly work-shy Kyle.

Stephen: His eyes are nice, aren't they?

Chris: We'd have a bit of Kyle. I'd be happy as Larry on that island.

Stephen: What, with him?

Chris: Yeah, I would. With them losing weight, it would make their willies look bigger. Or would you lose weight off your willy as well?

Stephen: Probably. Be like a peanut.

> 66
>
> Chris:
>
> ## With them losing weight, it would make their willies look bigger. Or would you lose weight off your willy as well?
>
> 99

We are all momentarily distracted by the possibility that Chris's cat Ginge is going to curl up on the same beanbag as incumbent basset hound Fred – it's like a scene from an advert for central heating or a pet shop.

Stephen: They've only known each other a couple of months.

Chris: If he gets on there, we'll have to take a picture.

Stephen: He'll forget why he came in in a minute, and go back out again.

Back to the archipelago-based action. Kyle seems to be actually sitting around on his arse on the beach – he's very much resting on the laurels of the fact that two weeks ago he started a fire with his glasses.

Stephen: Look at him: he's sitting there exfoliating his feet.

Chris: They're all going around bitching about him behind his back, but nobody's telling him to his face.

Stephen: Look how skinny he is. I'd love to go on there, lose some of this (slaps spare tyre). He looks older than twenty-eight, doesn't he? They look like corpses.

Chris: So they're not allowed anything? Sun cream? Aftersun? But they can leave the island at any time?

Stephen: They just do two weeks of starvation to lose weight and then say, 'Right, I wanna go now.'

One islander walks to waist height in the beautiful blue sea and goes for a number two.

Chris: I hope he uses Wet Wipes.

Stephen: What? Why would you shit in the sea? Dig a hole and shit in the hole!

Chris: If anything, I'd wanna be doing stuff because it would make the day go quicker. I'd be like, 'I'll make the camp look pretty.'

Stephen: You've already said your job, Chris.

Two of the men go on a hunt and discover a large deposit of 'actual shit' and one of them, an alpha Yorkshireman, remarks, 'What the fk is this? Jurassic Park?'**

Stephen: They're gonna get a crocodile.

'That is our dinner,' he says, when they espy what they think is a caiman.

Stephen: I don't think I'd wanna eat it, do you? [But] if I didn't see it killed, or being chopped up and cooked, and you just gave it to me, I probably would eat it.

Chris: I just don't know how they can bring themselves to actually kill things. I get really upset if I have to chop down a shrub. And they're not even alive, do you know what I mean?

Stephen: I hope it gets away.

It doesn't.

Chris: I don't wanna see this.

Stephen: Eurgh.

We cover our eyes. In rugby-club style, one of the men onscreen says, 'Gentlemen, we have handbags!' Another gives it the full 'Get in there, boys!'

Stephen: At least it was quick.

You could spend all day with this joyfully bickering double act, but Stephen has begged Chris to trim his hair at mate's rates and so I make my way back out into the blazing sunshine. Hairdressers usually ask you where you're going on holiday. If these two asked me, I'd say: 'Here, please.'

James Bond

Secret agent from the Cold War dragged into the post-Communist era and stripped of preposterous gadgetry and flying cars in order to compete with Jason Bourne; latest incarnation, the granite-like Daniel Craig as 'James Blonde', who hardly shags any Bond girls.

"

Leon:

The name's Bernicoff, Leon Bernicoff.

"

Rev. Kate: Bond looks like a sexy Tintin.

Giles: Isn't he famous for wearing budgie smugglers?

Rev. Kate: I'm always glad when the Bond villain isn't very attractive, because you don't want to have to fancy a baddie.

Tom Malone: I like Daniel Craig, he's not so suave and one-punch-and-you're-down – he gets hurt a bit and shows you do get damaged when you're James Bond. They've taken a few lessons off that Bourne, haven't they?

Leon: The name's Bernicoff, Leon Bernicoff.

Jamie Oliver

Everyone's favourite culinary wide boy. He's always got a show on and he always provokes strong reactions.

 Leon: He's all: 'Whack a bit of this in, whack a bit of that in.' I could slap him.

 Scarlett Moffatt: He's so posh.

 Betty Moffatt: He isn't.

 Scarlett Moffatt: Well, it's never things normal people would have in their kitchen – saffron, gold dust …

In February 2015, Jamie Oliver and his pal Jimmy Doherty presented a section of their show Friday Night Feasts, in which they suggested we should all be eating squirrel. So they put some in a pie and ate it in the garden.

 Amy Tapper: Why are they eating it outside? Why not eat it in the kitchen?

 Baasit Siddiqui: You know there's a bunch of squirrels in those trees thinking, you're eating Chester.

 Umar Siddiqui: Yeah, if it wasn't enough, let's go outside where the squirrels actually are and eat this in front of them.

 Ralf Woerdenweber: The English put everything in a pie. They're f**king perverts.

Japan

> ❝
>
> Chris:
>
> *You don't ever really see any fat ones, do you? They're all small.*
>
> ❞

 Leon: (makes culturally and geographically inappropriate cartoon kung fu noises)

 June: That's a bit racist.

 Leon: (beaming) I know.

 Chris: You don't ever really see any fat ones, do you? They're all small.

 Stephen: Gok Wan was fat.

 Chris: Yeah, he was.

Jeremy Clarkson

Pause-leaving motoring journalist turned golf-club god thanks to the success of Top Gear with those two other men; brought down like a Cotswold T-Rex by a politically correct cabal who don't like it when presenters hit producers because they can't get a steak after midnight. Stories about Clarkson have been all over the news the last few years, and our Goggleboxers all have their take on him.

 Leon: He's arrogant and insulting.

 Stephen: I just think anyone that passionate about cars has got something wrong with them.

 Rev. Kate: He thinks he's untouchable. He thinks he can say and do exactly what he likes.

 Mark Moffatt: He's old school. To him it's the norm.

 Scarlett Moffatt: Grandad's old school, but he doesn't go around thumping his employees.

 Chris: He's offensive in every way.

 Baasit Siddiqui: He's worse than Prince Philip.

 June: He thinks he's above the law.

 Ralf Woerdenweber: I know: he's arrogant, he is rude and he is a dickhead. But at the end of the day, he is *Top Gear*.

 Viv Woerdenweber: And he's a bit of a knob at times.

 Ralf Woerdenweber: He's too truthful. He says things the way they is.

 Stephen: I tell you what, why don't the BBC get him in a fast motor, cut the brakes. Problem solved; they can just rerun old ones over and over again.

 Chris: Or just get new presenters?

 Giles: He does represent a certain type of English attitude towards the world. And that is part of our history, therefore I feel that this sort of conspiracy to extinguish him, gag him, makes me feel rather sympathetic towards him. He causes

———— 66 ————

Giles:

The school bully. I think he suffers from low blood-sugar levels, which I suffer from, and it means he goes almost mad if he doesn't have a Snickers bar or something.

———— 99 ————

me a lot of amusement. The capers that he gets up to I do think are very funny. He's made you giggle, Nutty.

 Mary: I've never giggled in my life. I was rather shocked when he was on *Have I Got News for You* once and he got rather annoyed and he threw something at Ian Hislop in a rather vicious way. That shows another side to him.

 Giles: The school bully. I think he suffers from low blood-sugar levels, which I suffer from, and it means he goes almost mad if he doesn't have a Snickers bar or something.

 Rev. Kate: The only question is: will James May and Toad Hamster Boy continue without him?

Jeremy Paxman

Sneering ex-Inquisitor-General of question-repeating Newsnight legend, recently poached for Channel 4's election coverage.

 Dom: He's starting to look like a bloodhound.

 Steph: He looks like his face is melting. Like a candle.

 Stephen: Ooh, he frightens the life out of me.

 Chris: He's a horrible man.

 Stephen: He'd be like your head teacher, really miserable and horrible.

 Leon: Arrogant, rude and ill-mannered.

 Stephen: 'I'm Jeremy Paxman, a pompous git. I'm gonna make you feel small.'

 Jenny: He will ask the questions, he won't mince his words. He'll go for the jugular.

 Rev. Kate: You'd be absolutely bobbing it if you were a politician and you had to go up against Paxo. It's like throwing Christians to the lions, isn't it? He's going in to tear you apart.

Dom:

He's starting to look like a bloodhound.

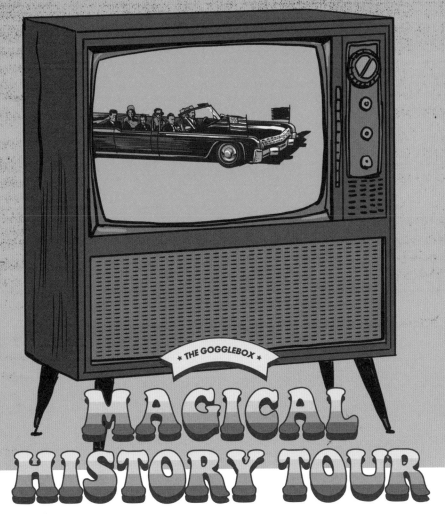

* THE GOGGLEBOX *

MAGICAL HISTORY TOUR

Through the power of TV, we take you back to 1963

John F. Kennedy, the assassination of

First Catholic President of the United States of America, the golden boy of the Democratic 'New Frontier' started the space race, diverted Armageddon and invented the Peace Corps.

He had to go. And did, in Dallas, November 1963, shot by one man from a number of angles. We watched the classic footage of the iconic motorcade.

Rev. Kate: It's still shocking, isn't it? Boom! It's amazing that he missed her. What's amazing about that is that she's in Chanel pink and she leans forward to look at her husband, what's going on? And then the head explodes. And even now, when we're so desensitized to violence on our TVs, you go, 'Woah!' When Lyndon Johnson was sworn in, she still had blood on her dress.

Jenny: They're still saying now that he never did it, you know.

Mark Moffatt: This is the ultimate conspiracy theory. Oswald probably didn't fire a bullet.

Tom Malone: You can see the bits come out of the back of his head.

Shaun Malone: Voldemort killed him.

Nikki Tapper: I never realized it was in the car.

Jonathan Tapper: Where have you been?

Josef: I remember exactly where I was. I was at Beaulieu, a late-night-dinner-cum-party. I happened to be downstairs at around midnight and my wife came down, crying her eyes out, and she said, 'Kennedy's been assassinated.' And I said, 'Don't be daft.' And she said, 'He has.' And I said, 'How do you know? You haven't got a radio.' And she said somebody had just driven in and told us. I said, 'No, I don't think it's true.' Of course it was. That's where I was and it's stuck in my mind ever since. It seemed so impossible.

Bill: I was doing something late at school and when I came home I went straight to Enfield Chess Club. And when I got there it was clear that something had happened. The guys there were talking about the Kennedy assassination, and I didn't know what they were talking about. I remember one guy saying, 'Well, he didn't do anything for me.' And I gradually put the information together.

June: Leon was going to decorate and his friend Bob was here to help him move the furniture in the bedroom, and his wife Marie and I were in the other room and I remember us shouting, 'Come down quickly! Kennedy's been assassinated!' and you wouldn't believe me. You couldn't make it up.

Leon: It was the Ku Klux Klan, and Southerners. Obviously. I'm amazed Obama's lasted so long. They're still there in the Southern states, aren't they?

June: They are overtly racist there. We were in Virginia and I was looking for jeans, and somebody was telling me where to go in the shopping mall, and we got a bus, and we were the only two whites on the bus. And I suddenly realized what it must feel like, you know, to be a minority.

Andrew Michael: A woman was asked on *Pointless*, 'Who did Lee Harvey Oswald shoot in Dallas?' And she answered, with a straight face, 'J. R. Ewing.' She thought it was the answer. (He turns to his wife to quiz her.) Who shot JFK then?

Carolyne Michael: Well, they said it was Lee Harvey Oswald.

Andrew Michael: I'm talking about in the wonderful world of Carolyne.

Carolyne Michael: He wanted to pull out of Vietnam, and I reckon the military-industrial complex wanted to stay in Vietnam. I think Johnson was behind it but the CIA probably did it.

Andrew Michael: And killing a bloke in a car is much easier than invading the Bay of Pigs.

Umar Siddiqui: You've watched all of the film *JFK*, haven't you? You started when you were eighteen and finished when you were twenty-one.

Baasit Siddiqui: I still haven't finished it.

Eve Woerdenweber: What, it was on TV, him being shot? Jesus!

Ralf Woerdenweber: It shocked the world.

Jon Snow

Cycling news anchor with coloured sock-and-tie fetish who's fronted Channel 4 News since the arse-end of Thatcherism and these days is most famous for having the same name as a Game of Thrones character.

Giles:

A motto to live by: try anything once. Apart from skunk. You see what it did to Jon Snow.

Carolyne Michael: We watch a lot of TV in the kitchen because we always eat together.

 Andrew Michael: *Channel 4 News* in the kitchen if it's dinnertime. It's a cornerstone. When I finally get to meet Jon Snow, I'm going to ask him about his socks and his ties. They're great.

 Louis Michael: I'm not going to lie, I have seen repeats.

 Alex Michael: How can he wear a different tie every day?

 Andrew Michael: The Queen wears a different outfit every day.

 Carolyne Michael: Not every time.

 Andrew Michael: What? The Queen's appeared in public in the same outfit?!

 Alex Michael: She rarely appears in public.

Andrew Michael: In fact I love Jon Snow so much, I fear I might be marginally homosexual.

 Alex Michael: What about Krishnan?

 Andrew Michael: Hmm, yeah. I like Krishnan, but it's not the same kind of man-love.

 Carolyne Michael: The thing is, Jon Snow wouldn't love you, because he's a pinko, isn't he?

Andrew Michael:

Do you know what? Jon Snow and I would be just great. Love can cross political boundaries.

 Andrew Michael: Do you know what? Jon Snow and I would be just great. Love can cross political boundaries.

 Louis Michael: Jon Snow is such a staple in my life, he's probably more of a father figure to me than my own dad.

 Andrew Michael: Ooh, I'm cut to the quick, Louis!

 Carolyne Michael: When we go out of the country, that's the one thing that we're happy about when we get back: oh, thank God, we can watch Jon Snow.

Andrew Michael: I hope he never retires. I'll be distraught.

In March 2015, as part of an experiment on the show Drugs Live, Jon Snow smoked skunk.

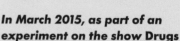 **Rev. Kate:** What's good is, it's a very, very serious show with a very, very serious news presenter about a very, very serious subject. But we're all just watching it cos it might be funny to see Jon Snow high.

On the screen, Jon Snow says: 'I feel woolly, I feel separated from myself. Not, not ... yes, a bit anxious.'

 Sandy: He needs some Bob Marley tunes with his smoking.

Giles: A motto to live by: try anything once. Apart from skunk. You see what it did to Jon Snow.

GOGGLEBOX TV

K

SPECIAL EDITION! Watching Kirstie and Phil with the Michaels!

Watching
KIRSTIE AND PHIL'S LOVE IT OR LIST IT
with THE MICHAELS

VOTE ANDREW

Exclamations fill the air when the Michael family get going. Vociferous dad Andrew, 55, forthright mum Carolyne, 54, outspoken Alex, 24, and passionate Louis, 18, are all strong characters with strong views, and when a remark sparks the blue touchpaper in their arena-like lounge, prepare for **CAPITAL LETTERS**.

Far enough out of central Brighton to give my conspiracy-theorist cab driver time to join the dots from the banking crisis to the Vatican, the Michaels' house proves to have no house number, so I wander lonely in the pink light of the magic hour until spotted by Alex, who beckons me up the drive.

❝

Louis Michael (on *Game of Thrones*):

I've been reading the books for ONE AND A HALF YEARS…

❞

Andrew, known colloquially as Andy, and Carolyne are retired hoteliers, and their well-appointed home gives the impression of an inviting guest house. In some ways it is, with three of their brood under its roof: the aforementioned, plus Katy, 26. (Eldest son Pascal, 21, is studying neuroscience at Aberdeen University.)

Having missed a series, the Michaels are chomping at the bit to get back in the saddle, and much of the verbal warfare that erupts tonight may simply be a release of pent-up armchair energy. While Carolyne makes the coffee and carefully times ahead to pizza o'clock, Andy lowers himself into his horizontal leather recliner, where he'll remain while food and drink is brought to him, the Alpha Dad (quite apt, a Greek letter for a Greek Cypriot).

Despite the substantial square footage, the family's tastes are not ostentatious and the atmosphere is make-yourself-at-home. A Jack Vettriano hangs next to a map of Cyprus. Like a judge at a marrow contest, I confirm that theirs is the biggest TV on *Gogglebox*, a 50-inch. 'Yay,' says Carolyne, politely. 'Size matters, you know!' shouts a triumphant Andy. Louis, bespectacled and with his hair pulled back, reminds us, 'Nowadays you can buy a 40-inch that's HD-ready for about £450.' Andy will not be silenced: 'There's a world of difference between 40 and 50 inches. A full TEN INCHES, in fact!'

Within minutes, the four of them are shouting over each other like a general election party-leaders' debate. A typical rally: Andy recommends I move to Eastbourne; Louis cries, 'Do NOT recommend the WORST place on the south coast!' Andy splutters, 'But it has the world-famous Carpet Gardens. I'VE GOT THE GUIDE BOOK!' You sense that Eastbourne's modest attraction is a recurring subject for discussion. Andy moves to caps lock: 'RECENTLY I ACTUALLY FOUND IN A JUNK SHOP A GUIDE BOOK FOR EASTBOURNE FROM 1964 AND IT SAID "THE WORLD-FAMOUS CARPET GARDENS"!' Louis raises the pitch rather than the volume: 'I could go and draw a picture of a rock and put "World-famous Rock" on it, but it's not official!' Carolyne Michael pops back in after checking on the pizzas. 'Can I hear raised voices?'

Louis is forced to raise his voice again when I broach the idea of watching an episode of *Game of Thrones* to tone up the family's invective muscles. 'I can't watch that!' he protests. 'I've been reading the books for ONE AND A HALF YEARS, and I've been waiting to watch the WHOLE SERIES! I don't even know what the characters look like! I'm saving the whole thing up. It's SO UNFAIR!'

'Have we got hidden chocolate?' Andy asks Carolyne discreetly. 'No,' she whispers. For all the bluster, he's soft-centred really.

With Game of Thrones clearly off the menu, Alex flicks gamely around the channels for a worthy replacement and the family just about agree on an episode of Kirstie and Phil, despite a few grumbles.

> Andrew:
>
> *There's a difference between 40 and 50 inches. A full TEN INCHES, in fact!*

Kirstie and Phil's Love It or List It

TUESDAY, 8PM

CH4 The home-owning nation's favourite third parties Phil Spencer ('I like moving house') and Kirstie Allsopp ('I hate moving house') represent stamp-duty-addicted 'Team List It' and improvement-biased 'Team Love It' respectively, tussling for the souls of dithering vendors.

Andrew Michael: (distracted) Oh, we've got that toilet seat!

Carolyne Michael: Everyone goes to B&Q.

Kirstie and Phil explain their separate briefs: to help a couple 'fall back in love' with their rubbish house, or to sell it and move on. The gladiatorial framework is pretty low-octane but the result is the same: nosing round other folks' houses.

Carolyne Michael: Everybody loves property porn. I think it's a very English phenomenon, this kind of programme. Anywhere else, if you told them you'd be interested in people looking around a house, they'd think it was the most idiotic programme. A bit like *Gogglebox* really – if you told them about it, they'd think it would never work. But why does it work?

Andrew Michael: Property-porn programmes haven't been as successful as *Gogglebox*, though.

Carolyne Michael: No, but there are a lot of them. They've proliferated.

Louis Michael: If you collated all the viewings of every property show . . .

Andrew Michael: I used to watch them years ago, but I'm tired of them now.

Louis Michael: I like them.

Andrew Michael: They're repetitive. But so is looking at houses in real life.

Carolyne Michael: We've all got a house. I think that everybody is just inherently curious. We just love looking at other people's houses, like, 'Ooh, look! I like the way they've made their bed!' I love to see what kettle they're using in the kitchen, or what carpet.

The couple Phil is currently showing round a 'really lovely house' are sent away so that he can lean into the camera and talk about them.

Andrew Michael: This little bit where they leave the room, I think it's a bit stupid.

Carolyne Michael: The other thing I don't understand is, why can't they find their own house?

Andrew Michael: IT'S A FUNDAMENTAL FLAW IN THE PROGRAMME AND NOBODY PICKS UP ON IT!

Carolyne Michael: All you have to do is look on the bloody internet and see all the houses.

Andrew Michael: If I wanted to find a house, why would I go to Phil? What can he do that I can't?

Louis Michael: He's a seasoned real-estate agent! He is! It's a fact!

Andrew Michael: He's not an estate agent, Louis.

According to Wikipedia, Phil studied as a surveyor. He used to be a professional home-finder, and these days he's a landlord and property investor.

Carolyne Michael: He's someone you would inherently trust.

Andrew Michael: I prefer that other one, I think her name's Amanda Lamb. She's quite sexy-wexy. I like Sarah Beeny as well. And do you know what, if Nigella Lawson went into the house-hunting business, I'd become a property developer. I would!

I interrupt to ask of Alex and Louis: 'How do you two younger people feel about watching a show about a market you may be locked out of?'

Alex Michael: I would never watch one. It's embarrassing being almost twenty-five and still living at home. (to her dad) Think of what you were doing at my age – you had your own business.

Andrew Michael: Yeah, but I was extraordinary.

Louis Michael:

We should all just live in the trees.

Alex Michael:

Let's just live in a treehouse, Louis.

Louis Michael: We should all just live in the trees.

Alex Michael: Let's just live in a treehouse, Louis.

Andrew Michael: You'll get cold.

Louis Michael: There are real, sustainable treehouses that use solar power, water, wind, everything, and they're all completely functional. It's actually a big space to live in! I don't know much about the property market but, when I do, I have the feeling it will be a sad revelation.

Carolyne Michael: Kirstie only ever, ever, ever wears skirts. I'd love to see her in some trousers.

Alex Michael: That's really sad that you pick up on that.

Carolyne Michael: I know.

Louis Michael: It's a woman's choice to wear what she likes.

Carolyne Michael: It is a bit mean, because you're right, this generation have been priced out of the market.

Louis Michael: Do they have the rocking horse we used to have?

Alex Michael: We still have. And its name is Pegasus.

Andrew Michael: (to Carolyne) You and I could do this job, and we could do it better!

'Not under your current contracts,' I say.

Louis Michael: You know the Kardashians? Kylie Jenner is my age and she bought a house for $2.7 million.

'It won't make her happy though,' I chip in.

Andrew Michael: It might.

Andrew very kindly gives me a lift back to Brighton station and exhibits expert navigational skills to deliver me to its back entrance, thus avoiding horrendous roadworks. But unlike a professional cab driver, he speaks with CAPS LOCK off, saving that for when he gets back home.

Carolyne Michael:

Kirstie only ever, ever, ever wears skirts. I'd love to see her in some trousers.

GOGGLEBOX
TV

Featuring
**THE LETTER
'L'**

Including
**LIFE AND
DEATH**

Plus
LITTLE ELSE

EXCLUSIVE! Discussing life and death with the Goggleboxers.

Life and Death

Life, and the end of it, come up a lot on *Gogglebox*.

Sid Siddiqui: It's strange, isn't it?

 Sid Siddiqui: It's strange, isn't it? How common is death, but how alien to us.

 Leon: It's so sad. My father was the first of the four to go. And I was so upset. I kept his dressing gown in my wardrobe and I'd stroke it at night.

 Steph: I would not want to wait till that point. I don't want the indignity of it.

 Dom: Don't worry. First time you shit yourself, you'd 'accidentally' fall out the window.

 Giles: That awful programme on Cambodia and Pol Pot's regime. I went into a decline when I watched that.

 Mary: They killed all the clever people. Pol Pot didn't like anybody with glasses.

Giles: That's me gone.

 Scarlett Moffatt: I'm scared of dying.

 Carolyne Michael: I hate that when people die. It's so shit.

Rev. Kate: I'm not afraid of dying.

Stephen: I'm in my element at the moment because this week's VE Day, and I like anything to do with World War Two.

>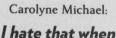
>
> Carolyne Michael:
>
> ## *I hate that when people die. It's so shit.*
>
>

 Chris: He loves anything to do with war.

 Stephen: I think it's because of my nan [that I'm interested in the era]: she lost her husband in World War Two, she brought up nine kids in East London on her own, and the spirit of her! She had such an amazing spirit; even when she was in her eighties, she was drinking, smoking, dancing and swearing like a trooper. I just loved her.

 Chris: And it's had a knock-on effect on who you are today. Because your mum is the way she is, and you're the way you are.

 Stephen: Even though it was the war, and the Blitz, there was a real sense of community. The best channel is Yesterday. It's always got stuff on about Hitler.

Chris: I can't stand all that. It's not that I'm not bothered. I'm very patriotic, as in I love being a British person and it's amazing what they all went through, and I don't think we should ever forget. But I don't want to watch twenty-six hours of it, and to be quite honest, I don't want to be reminded of the hideous stuff that people do to each other. What Hitler did to people was disgusting. I had to stop watching that movie *The Pianist* when they chucked the bloke in the wheelchair off the balcony. I was like, 'I'm not watching this.' Because it happened. And I don't want to watch it. I know it happened. I don't need to be shown it.

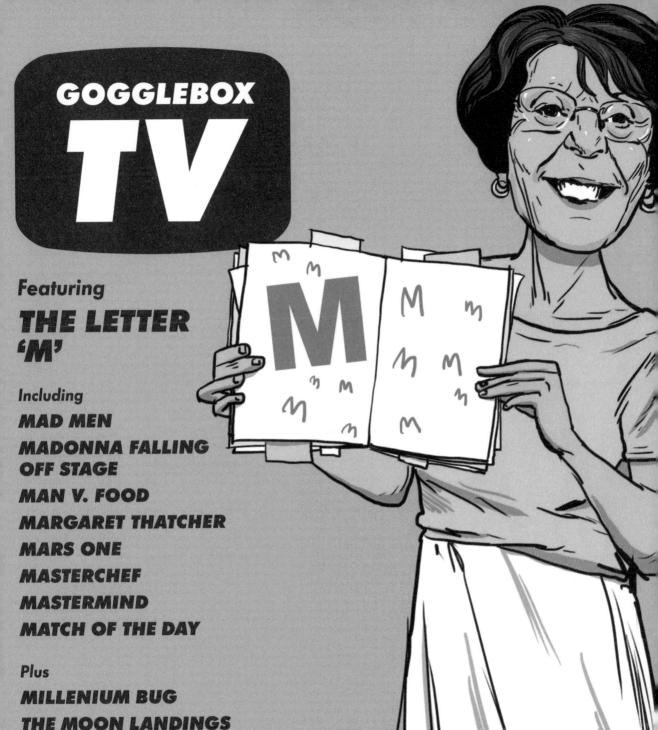

Mad Men

WEDNESDAY, IOPM

 SKY Critically adored, stylish and sexy period drama set in the world of New York advertising in the sixties and seventies.

 Giles: Didn't you used to work in advertising?

Mary: Yeah, but it wasn't like this. It was advertising for farm feed and corn pads.

MARY

Madonna Falling Off Stage

In February 2015, Madonna had a cape malfunction and was pulled off the stage of the Brit Awards by a backing dancer.

Stephen: They supersize everything though, innit?

Man v. Food

MONDAY, 9PM

FOOD NETWORK New Yorker Adam Richman attempts to eat massive platters of American food against the clock, ideally with nuclear chillies in. Because eating should be a race, not a sensual pleasure.

Chris: Have you ever been to America?

Stephen: No, never been. They supersize everything though, innit?

Chris: They are greedy bastards.

66

Rev. Kate:

Can you imagine if an alien from another planet landed on Earth and you showed them this? And you said: 'This is the most developed nation in the world – these are the world leaders. These are the people who are in charge of the planet, who have a finger on the button that could nuke us all. These are 'em. And look at them: stuffing their faces with pizza.'

99

Through the power of TV, we take you back to 1990

Margaret Thatcher, Prime Minister 1979–1990

Marmite prime minister and first woman in the top job, who either dragged Britain up off its knees and sold council houses, or cut out Britain's heart and sold council houses, depending on your viewpoint; all done chiefly by scaring the grey men in her Cabinet. In 1990, she made her last Commons appearance and defended her legacy. I sat down with the Goggleboxers to watch this iconic footage and talk about their take on the Iron Lady more generally.

Rev. Kate: She was so busy with her clipped vowels trying to deny her heritage. I still can't watch it. The first woman prime minister and that's what we got. Devoid of compassion. (shouts at the screen) Oh, shut the…! Someone called me a Marxist the other day, I was so proud.

 Jenny: I love Maggie Thatcher, I do. Go on, love!

 Lee: Get in there! This lady is not for turning.

 Jenny: I loved the way she dressed. She knew what to say, didn't she?

 Lee: John Major: he was grey, wasn't he?

 Jenny: Edwina Currie didn't think so.

 Mark Moffatt: She was a good orator.

 Scarlett Moffatt: So why did everybody hate her?

 Mark Moffatt: She closed all the mines.

 Betty Moffatt: I don't think, as a woman, you could do that job and not be like that. It wouldn't be every woman that could do it.

 Mark Moffatt: She demanded respect. She was a world leader.

 Scarlett Moffatt: It's like she's got marbles in her mouth.

 Jonathan Tapper: She was marvellous, Maggie. So powerful. Finchley was my constituency, but I wasn't old enough to vote. I was first able to vote in '87.

 Josh Tapper: I never realized how posh she was.

 Amy Tapper: I never realized that politics was such a big thing back then as well. Why did no one like her?

 Jonathan Tapper: A lot of people did like her. But she did make a couple of big mistakes.

> "

Shaun Malone:

I reckon, after Gaddafi, she's the most hated politician ever.

Tom Malone Jnr:

That's a strong thing to say, Shaun, considering Hitler and Stalin.

> "

I say, 'People who worked in the mines didn't like her.'

 Jonathan Tapper: (shouts) But Harold Wilson closed more mines than she did! It's double standards! (calms down) I wasn't having a go at you.

 Tom Malone Jnr: I think Maggie Thatcher's the reason why there have been hardly any female MPs compared to men.

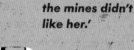

 Shaun Malone: I reckon, after Gaddafi, she's the most hated politician ever.

 Tom Malone Jnr: That's a strong thing to say, Shaun, considering Hitler and Stalin.

 Shaun Malone: Oh yeah, Hitler.

Tom Malone Jnr: She's hated up north.

 Shaun Malone: She's hated down south as well.

 Julie Malone: She's horrible. (shouts at TV) What about the miners?

Tom Malone: She's got such an aggravating voice.

 June: (with withering irony) My favourite politician.

 Leon: She was a cow. Her attitude was, 'My father made it, with his grocer's shop, so anybody should be able to do that.'

 June: She had such a strident voice, didn't she?

 Leon: She was a cow. She was a cow.

 June: And she did nothing for women, did she?

 Leon: What about the miners? June's father was a miner for fifty years.

 Stephen: I loved her.

 Chris: She was a bitch. But at least she kept things in order, didn't she?

 Stephen: But nowadays you don't see any rusty cars, do you? You've got Margaret Thatcher to thank for that. Quality control. No, it's true. I used to love the old scandals in the old days when an MP would get caught wearing stockings and suspenders.

 Chris: And a sheep running out of the room.

 Stephen: You don't get that now.

 Andrew Michael: It got worse under Tony Blair.

 Carolyne Michael: She took elocution lessons to lower her voice and sound more manly, didn't she?

 Andrew Michael: She's more scary than her *Spitting Image* puppet.

 Carolyne Michael: I actually liked Margaret Thatcher.

 Louis Michael: WHAT? OH MY GOD! Mum, people died of starvation in the north when she closed the mines!

 Carolyne Michael: I don't think they did, Louis. You've been watching too much *Billy Elliot*. She was the first female prime minister.

 Louis Michael: OH BIG F**KING WOW!

 Andrew Michael: I would have had a lot more time for her had she not sunk the *Belgrano*.

 Carolyne Michael: I agree, and I don't like the miners' strike, either.

> ❝
>
> Chris:
>
> ### *She was a bitch. But at least she kept things in order, didn't she?*
>
> ❞

Andrew Michael: I'm alright with the miners' strike.

Carolyne Michael: When we had the hotel in Bournemouth, she stayed there. We decorated the room she stayed in specially for her.

Louis Michael: You've never told me that one of the most famous prime ministers in British history stayed in your hotel!

Andrew Michael: It was a four-star. It was a decent hotel.

Carolyne Michael: We also had Kenneth Baker, Jeffrey Archer. They all came. I remember thinking, blimey, if the IRA bombed us they could hit half the flipping Cabinet.

Louis Michael: Why didn't you do it? You could have been the new Guy Fawkes.

Umar Siddiqui: This is almost like the argument David Cameron is having now.

Baasit Siddiqui: They're a rabble of toffs.

Sandy: She was the first lady, and the only one up to this day, babes.

Sandra: The Iron Lady!

Ralf Woerdenweber: England did really well under Margaret Thatcher, and I think lots of English people would love to have her back.

Viv Woerdenweber: The poor are even poorer now. The poor people's wages are going down.

Ralf Woerdenweber: The poor people are in hell, the rich people are in heaven, that's the gap.

Mars One

Non-profit, Dutch-funded initiative to put humans on the Red Planet by 2027. In February 2015, it was announced that 100 people had been selected to take part in the initial one-way trip.

Amy Tapper: Can you walk to Mars?

Viv Woerdenweber: Why would you go to Mars? There's nothing there.

Baasit Siddiqui: Do you reckon there are some people who entered that competition by accident, thinking the prize was a lifetime supply of Mars bars?

Scarlett Moffatt: He'll taste a sausage roll and say, 'Oh, it's like I'm on holiday in the Caribbean'.

MasterChef

WEEKDAYS, 8PM

BBC1 Durable cookery competition whose spin-offs (*Celebrity, The Professionals, Junior*) allow it always to be on, in one form or another, for ever, in perpetuity, seven nights a week, with Gregg Wallace all about the desserts. As the saying has it, 'Cooking doesn't get tougher than this.'

Stephen: I do like *MasterChef*, but I think they should change the judges. Gregg's boring. He's like an old barrow boy.

Dom: Who is this Wallace fella? He's a chef?

Steph: He's a cock.

Leon: 'I've never cooked in my life. But I'm judging you.' I would empty my pan over his head if I was there.

Jonathan Tapper: They're so annoying, they just stand over them while they've got so much pressure.

Leon: I tell you what, they'd have a piece of onion up their backside if I was cooking.

June: (shakes head)

Scarlett Moffatt: Everything's a party in his mouth. He'll taste a sausage roll and say, 'Oh, it's like I'm on holiday in the Caribbean: I'm lying on a beach, sipping a sangria.' You're eating a pie, what are you talking about?

Giles: Oh stick it in your mouth, you silly Charlie!

MASTERCHEF TV BINGO

Micro herbs!	A contestant who makes perfect food but leaves a filthy workstation	'She's a good, honest home cook'
Scallops on a bed of pea purée	Gregg: 'I could happily eat all of that'	Jon, of a celebrity: 'We know she can act, but can she cook?'
Something that takes fifteen minutes to set comes out of the freezer after four	Gregg: A past runner-up returns as a judge and lords it	Floods of tears from a contestant after being kicked out/winning the trophy/being told they are good at something for the first time

June: He's like an advert for toothpaste now, Gregg Wallace.

 Leon: All he's been is a stall-holder.

 Baasit Siddiqui: There's something very asexual about John Torode. I think he goes home and sleeps with a turnip. As for Gregg, more and more of his shirt buttons are coming undone.

 Sid Siddiqui: And his head's getting shinier and shinier.

 Baasit Siddiqui: That's how you know if Gregg finds you attractive.

 Umar Siddiqui: You can see yourself in his head.

 Leon: Just wait until they see my curry.

 June: For goodness' sake, stop talking about your curry. It's not that good.

 Tom Malone: Sausage, mash and beans. What's the matter with that?

 Stephen: The thing is, these programmes, they make you feel hungry, don't they?

 Chris: Not when they're dishing up things that look like f**king shit, they don't.

" "

Baasit Siddiqui:

There's something very asexual about John Torode. I think he goes home and sleeps with a turnip.

" "

Sandra: You have to be in the dark. It's always been in the dark.

Mastermind

FRIDAY, 8PM

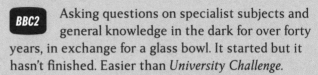

BBC2 Asking questions on specialist subjects and general knowledge in the dark for over forty years, in exchange for a glass bowl. It started but it hasn't finished. Easier than *University Challenge*.

Steph: That music!

Josef: It's got the right name: 'Approaching Menace'.

Sandy: Do you think they have it dark cos you're supposed to think better?

Sandra: You have to be in the dark. It's always been in the dark.

" Baasit Siddiqui:

He looks a bit like Gollum, doesn't he?

"

Josef: Apparently they got the idea for this from the war, when people were being interrogated. [They thought] why not have an interrogation which is in a friendlier atmosphere?

 Bill: Not much friendlier.

 Ralf Woerdenweber: I think, in real life, these people are really, really, really, really boring.

 Carolyne Michael: How long has this programme been going on? That Magnus Magnusson doesn't look any different. He looks exactly the same.

 Andrew Michael: That's John Humphrys.

 Leon: I met John Humphrys at my seventieth.

 Dom: Isn't he a lovely guy? I bet he's got a pocket full of Werther's Originals.

 Baasit Siddiqui: He looks a bit like Gollum, doesn't he?

 Carolyne Michael: The questions are so long, I've forgotten the beginning before he's even got to the end.

 Sandra: I knew that!

 Sandy: Why you never said it, then?

 Sandra: Too fast.

 Bill: I've often wondered if I'm getting more knowledgeable as I get older or if *Mastermind* is getting easier.

 Josef: All the questions are easy if you know the answer.

 Leon: I've had a glass of wine, which dulled my senses.

 June: Yes, you'd have answered them all otherwise.

Rev. Kate: All the pressure, all that stress and all they get is a glass bowl.

 Scarlett Moffatt: That's a bit of a shit prize.

 Dom: What they should do is tell them they can take the chair home. Nobody wants the damn vase.

66

Josef:

Apparently they got the idea for this from the war, when people were being interrogated.

99

Match of the Day

SATURDAY, 10.45PM

BBC1 The BBC's main football show. In 2014, it celebrated its fiftieth anniversary. It is currently presented by crisp-peddling ex-England international Gary Lineker.

Leon: I love *Match of the Day.*

 Baasit Siddiqui: I think he's slowly but surely turning into Des Lynam, isn't he?

 Leon: I love *Match of the Day*. Unless Everton lose, and then I don't watch it. (on Gary Lineker) He's always making a joke of things and laughing and sneering; I cannot stand the man. Very big ears.

 Sandra: Crisps!

 Jonathan Tapper: He's easy on the eye, [but] I wouldn't call him good-looking. I'm not particularly attracted to him.

 Josh Tapper: You're more of a Jamie Redknapp man.

Watching
MEET THE SLOTHS
with BILL AND JOSEF

 I arrive at Bill's house in Cambridge on the day of the general election. He swings the front door wide, shouting, 'Liberal Democrats? Sorry, not interested!' and affects to slam it in my face. I've been framed.

The seasoned journalist, author and former chess champion, 68, proves temperate company on a politically stormy afternoon. A washing machine chugs hypnotically in the basement kitchen, occasional drilling is heard from next door and a mannerly

Bill:

Meet the Sloths *sounds like it's going to be a comedy programme.*

carriage clock chimes on the half-hour to keep us from losing track of time (something that's always a possibility in the balmy university city). Many assume he shares the split-level pad with his old friend Josef, 70, but the married accountant with a board-game habit has always lived in Southampton, hence the Hampshire burr.

'I used to see him two, three times a year, maybe,' says Josef, wearing a particularly busy Hawaiian shirt. 'In the last two or three years, we've met more times than we had in the previous fifteen.'

'Shall I turn Haydn off?' shouts Bill, before muting whichever of the Austrian composer's symphonies is serenading us and setting down before me a mini cafetière. Josef regales us with a tale of being recognized on a cruise ship by a woman who refused to believe he wasn't on *The Vicar of Dibley* (the rum old sort who says, 'No, no, no-no-no, no, no, no-no' *ad infinitum*), and another of how a local reporter in equally dogged pursuit keeps asking him for Scarlett Moffatt's address. 'I say, I'm not giving it to you for two reasons: one, it would be breaking a confidence, and two, I don't have it.' I admire his moral fibre but Bill asks if he'd submit under torture. 'If they were torturing me, I'd make up an address.'

Before you ask, the huge canvas of the woman struggling with her jumper does indeed follow you around the room. It was painted using oil and acrylic by a former neighbour of Bill's, the artist Rebecca Ivatts, who's cannily selling limited-edition prints of it on her website. (Her parents still occasionally park outside Bill's house.) The art is offset on the opposite wall by what Bill refers to as his 'sloth-of-the-month calendar'. The Central and South American tree mammal which moves at a sensibly unhurried pace is Bill's favourite animal. I think it reflects well upon a man if he has a favourite animal. A trio of cuddly sloths in human form proceed to share the oatmeal sofa.

Sticklers for order and known attendees of the Mind Sports Olympiad, Bill and Josef, the latter once an editor of the *Scrabble Dictionary*, trade examples of poor grammar and questionable usage for sport. Josef saw a sign on holiday whose creative use of the apostrophe he couldn't wait to tell Bill about: 'Duc'ks eggs'. Bill recalls the time he used to live in Highbury in north London and habitually met Boris Johnson on the bus when he was still at the *Telegraph*: he heard the future London mayor call the newspaper to correct a column he'd delivered, asking the sub-editor to change 'encomium' to 'valedictory'. Bill glows with pride: 'Not only did he know the difference, he cared enough to change it.'

In order to fully immerse ourselves in an episode of *Meet the Sloths*, we place a furry toy sloth on each of our laps,

and settle down with the neighbour's drill still whirring in the background.

Before we begin, we have a discussion about the pronunciation of the word 'sloth'. The OED says 'sloth' with a long 'o', to rhyme with 'both', but many – including the Americans who work at the sloth sanctuary in the programme we're about to watch – rhyme it with 'cloth'. Bill, a sloth devotee who has cuddly sloths, sloth mugs and a sloth calendar in his house, quotes the linguistic book Wordwatching by Alex Horne: Horne ruminates that the deadly sin sloth is mentioned less 'possibly because of confusion about its pronunciation'.

Meet the Sloths

WEDNESDAY, 8PM

 A dewy-eyed documentary from the self-explanatory Animal Planet Channel set in 'a sleepy corner of Costa Rica' at the world's only sanctuary for orphaned and injured sloths, designed to elict responses as varied as 'Oooh' and 'Ahhh'.

Bill: *Meet the Sloths* sounds like it's going to be a comedy programme. Sloths are the masters of an alternative lifestyle. I'm told they can scamper around the canopy of the rainforest pretty quickly.

The narrator of the documentary begins: 'Meet baby sloth Toby, rejected by his mother and kicked out of a tree. He landed in the right place.'

Bill: It's fantastic what they've done with this place.

Josef: Have you been to Marwell Zoo in Hampshire? The meerkats down there get out sometimes. The keepers don't mind – they go home when they feel like it.

Another baby sloth, Buttercup, is found clinging to her dead mother. 'As soon as she saw the kooky American lady with a passion for animals, she knew she was safe.'

Bill: Eurgh, soppy commentary.

Josef: He's got no time for this.

Bill: Don't like this anthropomorphic bollocks. The documentary is about the sanctuary, not about the sloths. Look at those claws! They're wonderful! Did you see my sloth-of-the-month calendar?

I did. It's in pride of place above the mantel; hard to miss. May's sloth is … a sloth.

Josef: We went to Colchester Zoo and saw sloths there. And I thought, you really are lazy sloths. They had their claws hanging on the pole, but it was just the right height so they weren't actually hanging, they were lying there. They were just giving the impression of hanging!

Hence their name.

Bill: They're so badly designed for life on Earth.

The three-fingered Bradypus sloth has 'a medieval haircut, and a rather enigmatic Mona Lisa smile'. The two-fingered variety, Choloepus, is described as 'a cross between a Wookie and a pig'.

Josef: I can see that. This is what's so unfair about some animals – they've got the 'cute' aspect, hence they're more popular than those that haven't.

Bill: I had a lovely e-romance with a very devout Christian a few years ago, and at one stage she sent me a copy of *The Everlasting Man* by G. K. Chesterton, a piece of Catholic apologia. So I sent her back a parody I'd written called *The Everlasting Bradypus* by G. K. Chestersloth, explaining how a sloth was quite obviously God's chosen creature. I was very pleased with that. The most obvious reason was that God placed the sloth upside down in the canopy so that it would always be looking up into the heavens to face its creator. And also, coming down once a week to poo, it left the rest of the mammals scampering around in its toilet, so it's quite clearly literally and metaphorically above the other creatures.

Have you ever touched a sloth?

Bill: No, I've never seen a sloth. I once emailed London Zoo and asked if I could come and interview their sloth, and they seemed in favour of it, but I didn't hear back from them. I will one day go and meet their sloth. They flew over a girl sloth as a mate and after some time she became pregnant, much to the surprise of the keepers, as they hadn't even realized the two sloths had acknowledged each other's existence! They got on with it when no one was watching.

Do they have a voice?

Bill: They squeak, yes. The extent of the sloth vocabulary is one of the things we don't know about.

Josef: Have you been to Monkey World down in Dorset? That started out as a sanctuary for badly treated monkeys. We went there. It's got tall fences but no roof. I said, 'Pardon me for saying so, but you seem to be extremely naive: monkeys climb trees. All they've got to do is climb the trees and they're out.' And they told me, 'They do get out, and sometimes go down into the

> **Bill:**
> ## *Look at those claws! Did you see my sloth-of-the-month calendar?*

Sloth of the month
calendar
2015

village, but they always come back. They've got heated premises and guaranteed food! We've never lost a monkey!'

Bill: Have you seen the clip of David Attenborough talking to a sloth? It is absolutely beautiful. He climbs up a ladder and he's face to face with a sloth.

How do you feel about zoos?

Josef: I have mixed feelings. You may be doing it for the right reasons, to protect species and reintroduce them to the wild, but shouldn't you be tackling the fact that other humans are destroying the wild? It's like this idea of trying to recreate a mammoth. It's gone. Forget it. The other thing with zoos is that they artificially switch day and night so you can see nocturnal animals, and you see kids banging on the glass. I want to clip them round the ear.

Someone from the sanctuary makes some visiting kids coo by bringing out, literally, a bucket of baby sloths.

Josef: Again, it's typical: it's always the young, cute ones.

Bill: It's good that they only allow the public in once a week. I've just finished writing a sequel to my *Things That Nobody Knows* book, and it has five sloth-related questions.

"

Bill:

I once emailed London Zoo and asked if I could come and interview their sloth, and they seemed in favour of it, but I didn't hear back from them.

"

The clock strikes half past for the final time on my visit. Divided only by an appreciation (Bill's) of opera, the two long-distance jousters make the world a more precise place. Taking my cue, I exit, pursued by a sloth, who will, frankly, never catch me.

HELLO

★ THE GOGGLEBOX ★

MAGICAL HISTORY TOUR

Through the power of TV, we take you back to 1999

The Millennium Bug, New Year's Eve

Would the world economy collapse and planes fall out of the sky because your microwave was never programmed to go from 99 to 00 on the stroke of midnight? Spoiler alert. We watched one of the many scare pieces that were broadcast in the lead-up to the millennium.

Rev. Kate: Do you remember that? 'The microwave won't work. Oh no!'

Graham: (referring to the *Sky News* recreation of some bacon failing to be microwaved) Who cooks bacon in a microwave? No television. No bacon. It's not that long ago, but it seems so dated, it's terrifying.

Rev. Kate: It's like a comedy sketch. It's *The Day Today*. This is genius. Serious news face.

Scarlett Moffatt: I remember you going round all the house, pulling all the plugs out before we went out.

Betty Moffatt: Well, you can't take chances, not with the Millennium Bug!

Scarlett Moffatt: I don't want me telly turning into a friggin' Transformer!

Mark Moffatt: It's mad that we all fell for that. It's the media telling us it's going to happen and we believe it.

Andrew Michael: It was so bad that the Chinese government actually told the heads of the Chinese airlines, 'You have to be in the air, in the planes, at midnight on 31 December,' and that's how they ensured that nothing would go wrong. Can you imagine how much effort they put into making sure there wasn't a computer meltdown?

Alex Michael: The computers were cleverer than people thought.

Andrew Michael: And, if you watch *Terminator*, you'll know that the computers take over.

Louis Michael: I think the machines would do a better job than us anyway. We're retards.

Baasit Siddiqui: Who microwaves bloody bacon?

Umar Siddiqui: I'm glad we can laugh about this now, cos it could have gone the other way.

Baasit Siddiqui: If the Millennium Bug was an issue, the last thing you'd be worried about is your bloody alarm clock!

Sid Siddiqui: Did they not ground all the planes? If they were that serious, they'd have grounded them.

Umar Siddiqui: A plane's not going to suddenly think, hang on, it's the year 0000, I haven't been invented yet!

Baasit Siddiqui: Do you remember what my summer job was? I worked for the IT department at the hospital and my job was to go around installing anti-Millennium Bug software. I spent the whole summer doing it. It was definitely bullshit; whoever made the program must have made a fortune. God knows what it did. Dad worked for the estates department, which is all fancy computers that controlled the central heating in the hospital and all the valves and stuff, and whatever I installed really messed up the whole hospital.

Sid Siddiqui: It took months to recover. So it did have an effect!

Sandy: I just thought to myself, do you know what? Everything's going wrong anyway. That's life. If it's gonna happen, it's gonna happen. It's human nature, babes. Things do go wrong.

Sandra: It never affected me. They would have sorted it all. This is England, man.

Viv Woerdenweber: There was people digging underground shelters and filling them up with big bottles of water and supplies. Richard and Judy were on *This Morning* and he believed it and he was stocking up and he was saying, 'It's a real threat, it's a real threat.' And people moved house! They moved to Scotland where there was no electricity because they thought the world was going to collapse! Seriously. We went to New Brighton, to a party, for New Year's Eve and then we went on the prom and everyone had champagne, and they were all waiting with their mobile phones to see if they'd still work at midnight, and the network jammed because everyone was on their phones!

Through the power of TV, we take you back to 1969

The Moon Landings

The space race was over when, on 21 July 1969, Neil Armstrong walked on the Moon and fumbled his 'giant leap for mankind', leading to more conspiracy theories about it being faked than were generated by the final of this year's *Britain's Got Talent*. We watched the classic footage and a healthy debate ensued.

Rev. Kate: He fluffed his lines there, didn't he? He was supposed to say, 'One small step for this man.' Imagine crowding round the telly to watch that for the very first time. They've never been back, have they?

 Graham: I think it's pretty well established that they went there.

 Rev. Kate: Who filmed it? Did they get off and set up the camera, then get back on the pod? So it is faked in a way.

 Lee: Ooh, I was only one. I might have been watching it.

Armstrong comments that the Moon 'looks beautiful' and 'very pretty'.

 Lee: How can it look beautiful? Very *pretty*? You're seeing something we aren't.

 Jenny: I can't believe they can put a man on the Moon, but they can't cure cancer. With the technology they had then, and what we've got now, they still can't cure cancer. (she thinks for a moment) Didn't they have a problem?

No, that was Apollo 13.

 Lee: *They* had a problem.

 Jenny: So that's forty-eight years ago.

 Lee: It's a long time, isn't it?

 Scarlett Moffatt: It's not real. Is it, Dad? There's no atmosphere, but the flag was waving. There's shadows. And the shadows are all wrong, aren't they? And there's a picture of a rock and it's got a letter or a number on it. They say it's a prop.

 Betty Moffatt: Why would they want to imply that they went?

 Scarlett Moffatt: Because America wanted to beat ... is it Russia?

 Mark Moffatt: It was the Cold War.

 Scarlett Moffatt: How, with all the technology that we have now, can we not just make it straight up there when we apparently did that in the 1960s when not many people even had colour televisions? It makes no sense.

 Mark Moffatt: When it's night on Earth, you can see stars. When it's night on the Moon – and it's night all the time – you can't see any stars.

 Scarlett Moffatt: You can see in one of the photos, reflected in his visor, that they're in a set.

 Betty Moffatt: That upsets me, that. I just thought it was real. I like to think it's real.

 Mark Moffatt: You wouldn't dare come forward – you'd fear for your life.

 Scarlett Moffatt: Honestly, we have not been to the Moon. People might say that me and me dad are stupid, but I think people are more stupid if they believe what they see. No one questions it. We should question it. It's like, Ebola was massive and now we never hear about it – it's because it's to cover up other things. That's why people like Miley Cyrus are put here.

 Mark Moffatt: Ebola's there so that Britain and America can check everybody that comes into the country.

Do you go as far as 9/11 being known about in advance?

 Scarlett Moffatt: Yeah. A couple of weeks before, the man who owned the building insured it against terrorists, when no one had really heard of terrorists before. They had to put fear into everyone again. It meant that Americans didn't want to leave America, because they didn't want to go on planes. And it looks like the demolition of a building.

And I can't understand why nobody seems to mind that America have got a whole area, Area 51, that no one knows anything about and you're not allowed on Google Maps or anything, and everybody seems fine with it – 'Oh yeah, it's Area 51.'

Giles: I was at prep school in North Wales, classic Evelyn Waugh style, and we were all gathered in front of the one television in the headmaster's study, and all the boys were watching it.

Mary: I think we stayed up to watch it, because in those days you couldn't replay it – you had to be there. It should have been astounding, because in those days, pre-cynicism, pre-conspiracy theory, one accepted that it was true. And now I'm wondering, was it true?

Giles: A lot of people think it was a fake.

Mary: To make the Russians think they were ahead of them?

Giles: I would've thought they could have got minerals from the Moon. There must be money in it for someone.

Julie Malone: If it was faked, I think somebody who was in on it would have come out by now.

 Tom Malone Jnr: Maybe Kennedy was in on it. Oh no, that was before, wasn't it? (pause) There was people at Cape Canaveral who saw the rocket go up.

 Shaun Malone: If it was faked, somebody could sell their story for billions.

 Tom Malone Jnr: You could probably land on the Moon with the technology that's in my phone.

 Shaun Malone: Our PlayStation is probably cleverer than that.

 Josh Tapper: Were you alive when this happened?

 Jonathan Tapper: No.

 Josh Tapper: Yes, you were.

 Jonathan Tapper: Oh yeah, 1969. I was two.

 Amy Tapper: I think this was staged, honestly.

 Josh Tapper: I think so too.

 Jonathan Tapper: So do I. I'm very sceptical about it. They showed the first craft landing on the Moon. Well, who took film of that? And have they landed on the Moon since? Because if they could have done, they'd be there now, exploring the place.

 June: I just couldn't visualize from here to the Moon. My mind would not comprehend it. I'm still going to believe it's true.

 Stephen: It didn't happen, did it?

 Chris: Something to do with the shadows.

― 66 ―

Scarlett Moffatt:

You can see in one of the photos, reflected in his visor, that they're in a set.

― 99 ―

Stephen: How haven't they filmed anyone else walking on there ever since?

 Chris: Just imagine being famous for something that never really happened!

 Louis Michael: I've never seen this.

 Alex Michael: I've never seen this.

 Carolyne Michael: I remember the whole school sitting there on benches watching it.

 Andrew Michael: Let me clarify it: that's the lunar excursion module and when the two astronauts, Buzz Aldrin and Neil Armstrong, go back, they go up and dock with the command module, containing Michael Collins, which is going round. The top part of the lunar excursion module jettisons off and goes up, and it leaves the legs behind. You get the most powerful telescope on Earth, you point it to the Sea of Tranquillity, and you can't find the base of the lunar excursion module, which makes me a little bit suspicious.

 Louis Michael: If it's a lie, it's one of the biggest lies ever. So what moron had jurisdiction over this project that they left so many blatant plot holes?

 Umar Siddiqui: This is what TV is about.

 Sid Siddiqui: Until then, the Moon was still thought of as a big cheesecake.

Moon Landings Fun Fact

20 men have walked on the Moon in total.

 Baasit Siddiqui: (on Neil Armstrong's famous words) He didn't think of that off the top of his head, though, did he?

 Sid Siddiqui: (on repeat visits to the Moon) Why would they want to go there for a second time? There isn't anything fascinating there to go for.

 Baasit Siddiqui: Was it a case of 'been there, done that'?

 Sid Siddiqui: It was something you'd never imagine in your wildest dreams. It was remarkable at that time that we could talk to them on the Moon.

 Baasit Siddiqui: My signal's that crap I can't even talk to you and you're only twenty streets down. They were definitely not on the EE network.

 Sandy: It was dodgy, babes. That was a set-up in a studio! Where there should have been a shadow, there was no shadow, and where there shouldn't have been a shadow, there was a shadow.

 Eve Woerdenweber: Someone's got the Hoover on in the background and it's in the friggin' studio. Look! He's walking like he's shit himself.

 Ralf Woerdenweber: This was something that nobody ever managed to do.

 Viv Woerdenweber: If they had done a Moon landing and walked on the Moon, why hasn't anybody else done it since?

 Ralf Woerdenweber: Because they don't have to do it. And there's loads of money involved. And what can we see that we don't know already?

 Viv Woerdenweber: I personally think it was a load of waffle.

Murder Mystery

Old pals Lee and Jenny often holiday together and sometimes share a room, Morecambe and Wise-style. (Lee: 'People thought we were a married couple when we went to Benidorm – the maid came in and said, "*Hola!* You on honeymoon?"'). But their abiding passion, before *Gogglebox* recognition made such pastimes impractical, was attending organized murder-mystery weekends. Jenny's husband, Ray, and, Lee's partner, Steve, used to book them as presents for the pair, who always threw themselves into the proceedings with their customary gusto.

 Jenny: It's like being in a TV detective show. The last one we went to, people thought we were the actors. Wherever we stay, we have to be near a Wetherspoons.

 Lee: She fell asleep on the table last time. Whenever we go, people want to sit with us because we get right into it, right from the off.

 Jenny: When I leave my house, whatever the theme is, I'm in that theme.

 Lee: I say to her, 'You aren't getting on the train with me!'

 Jenny: We did a 1950s one: Lee was a spiv, I had this bright ginger wig with all me hair in a net round the back, a real fur coat, and I was carrying a suitcase and wearing a bottle-green dress I'd sent away for off the internet.

 Lee: I'm getting on the train with her and everybody's looking and going, 'Is that a tranny?'

 Jenny: I went to one as Sherlock Holmes. I had a big magnifying glass. I never get the murderer right, but when I come home and tell Ray, he gets it straight away. We did this *Father Ted* one.

 Lee: I was the Pope.

Jenny:

It's like being in a TV detective show. The last one we went to, people thought we were the actors. Wherever we stay, we have to be near a Wetherspoons.

 Jenny: He looked fantastic. And I was a nun. The guy who played the old priest – Father Jack – he was good. Ooh, I felt sick. He had all this earwax.

 Lee: We've been to that many, we started to see the same cast.

 Jenny: We did 'Who Killed Elvis?' He was Elvis – he's won the best-dressed about three times. On the night, we'd gone back up to the hotel, and it was a no-smoking room.

 Lee: I said, 'Go in the shower, turn it on, and have a ciggy in there.'

 Jenny: So I did. The alarms went off.

Lee: She was running round the room with this cig, going, 'F**kin' 'ell, I've set the alarms off.'

 Jenny: When I came back out of the bathroom, he was on the bed with his Elvis suit on. That was brilliant.

 Lee: Oh yeah, there was a wedding in the same hotel as the murder mystery once and somebody got 'killed' on the stairs. And of course this bride was going ballistic!

 Jenny: It had frightened her to death.

 Lee: What was that one where I was an officer and a gentleman? I went outside for a cigarette and these people were having a Christmas party, and these two girls said, 'Oh, are you the stripper?'

GOGGLEBOX TV

N

Featuring
THE LETTER 'N'

Including
NATURAL HISTORY

NIGELLA LAWSON

NINJA WARRIOR

Plus
NOAH

Natural History

Leon: I love meerkats.

 Alex Michael: Name an animal that's sexier than a lion.

 Stephen: I always just feel sorry for whatever's being chased.

 Leon: I hate animals. All animals, except for cats.

 Amy and Josh Tapper: I hate cats.

 Carolyne Michael: I have an actual phobia of snakes. I love bears, though.

 Leon: I don't like whales. Too big.

 Dom: I kissed a dolphin. And I liked it.

 Leon: I love meerkats.

Nigella Lawson

Suggestively finger-licking TV cook whose child-bearing shape and come-to-Waitrose eyes combine to transfix mostly middle-aged men with no interest in cooking.

Child-bearing shaped.

Leon:

Very attractive, Nigella. Well busted.

 Carolyne Michael: I'm not sure I want to watch her. I might get jealous.

 Andrew Michael: How can anybody be that gorgeous?

 Rev. Kate: She's ever so pleased with herself, isn't she? Mind you, I would be too if I looked like that.

> Steph:
>
> *She gets on my tits.*
>
> Dom:
>
> *I'd like to see that.*

 Jonathan Tapper: Very subtle hands.

 Leon: It didn't stop her husband trying to strangle her.

 Leon: Very attractive, Nigella. Well busted.

 June: (sighs)

 Steph: I've never liked her.

 Dom: I actually thought she was quite pretty when she had the dodgy teeth.

 Steph: Cos your mother's got a dodgy tooth, that's why.

 Dom: Oh.

 June: She doesn't just throw the herbs in. She almost fondles them and drops them in.

 Leon: She's like you, love. You're better-looking.

 Dom: Are you sure you're not jealous?

 Steph: What's there to be jealous of? Don't envy her cooking. Don't envy her looks. Don't envy her marriage. Don't envy her father.

 Dom: Her hair?

 Steph: I don't envy her hair. That's thin hair made to look fluffy.

NIGELLA LAWSON TV BINGO

Plumptuous	Squeeze	Blowout
Heady	Flesh	Sensual
Juices	Messy	Stiff

Watching
NINJA WARRIOR
with THE MALONES

 In a house in the back corner of a cul-de-sac in one of Manchester's outlying suburbs live four Rottweilers and one Staffordshire bull terrier. If you don't like dogs, or prefer ones that fit in handbags, this is not a good destination for you. (A letterbox has been fixed to the outside of the house so that the postman needn't approach the front door.) Me? I can't wait to meet them all.

On the morning I rock up, I'm surprised when the door is opened by a human man. Perhaps he is the dogs' butler? (I later discover that one of the

> ##
> Tom Malone Jnr:
> ### *I'm basically a ninja already.*
> ##

Rottweilers, Izzy, can open all of the interior doors in the house by herself.) He is in fact the voluble and witty Tom Malone, 50, who explains that the dogs are out the back and delivers me to the *Gogglebox* room, where the only non-human is a knitted PG Tips monkey.

Tom works 'on the roads', but scrubs up nicely in a crisply ironed checked shirt and what appear to be box-fresh trainers. His wife Julie, 52, usually seen without her specs, describes herself as 'taxi driver, cook, cleaner, washer, ironer, gopher, dog-walker and decorator'; brothers Tom Jnr, 21, a dance teacher and proud member of a Hartlepool hip-hop dance crew, and Shaun, 20, a volunteer football coach, complete the quartet.

Tom works 'funny hours', but it was Tom Malone Jnr who, after a long night celebrating the end of another series of *Gogglebox*, rolled in at 6.30am and understandably takes a while to warm up. His T-shirt speaks for him: 'Dance is a universal language'.

The Malones – the only household on my tour serious enough about TV to have a wall-mounted flatscreen – are all about their dogs, whose human names (Dave, Bob, Frank, Izzy and Lucy) are designed to make them seem less frightening when they're out in the park. Before they let the dogs in – incrementally, one by one, so they can get used to the visitor in their midst – Tom Malone tells me he spent his first seven years in Kilmeage, Co. Kildare, in Ireland, where he developed a phobia of nuns. 'He's wary of penguins as well,' chips in Tom Jnr, gradually emerging from his top night out.

When setting up my camera for a self-timed photo, Julie offers me the box containing their last dog's ashes to stand it on. 'Joe won't mind,' she assures me. Joe died just before Christmas, when latest arrival Bob, now the size of a hatchback, was still a puppy.

The Malones are a loquacious lot and their house is warmly welcoming – I'm served amazing toasted sandwiches containing beans and halloumi cheese, and when Dave knocks over my coffee, it's cleaned away and replaced with zero fuss. You can feel the adoring, respectful deference to animals in the air. Tom was driving his wagon to Wigan once and stopped to rescue a ferret from under a car, which ran up inside his shirt. They bought it a hutch and food, then found out it was dying, but were happy to have improved the quality of its life even for a short time.

Tom Jnr says, 'When we'd been naughty, growing up, Mum would say to us, "If I'd had dogs before kids, we never would have had you."' She didn't mean it, of course, but you get her drift.

With Dave snoozing hard on my feet, I'm unable to switch seats without disturbing him at a pivotal stage in our friendship, so I lean in from the left as we limber up for an episode of Ninja Warrior.

Ninja Warrior

SATURDAY, 7.30PM

ITV An indoor-arena version of a Japanese obstacle-course game show, presented by identi-host Ben Shephard, former midfielder Chris Kamara and ex-Saturdays pop star Rochelle Humes, and staged at what used to be called G-Mex, now Manchester Central. Obstacles include Quintuple Steps, Dancing Stones (a sort of giant-mushroom-jumping challenge), Rope Junction and Warped Wall. Some involve falling in the water. Partisan hyperventilation and foam hands the size of the Malones' dogs are encouraged among the audience.

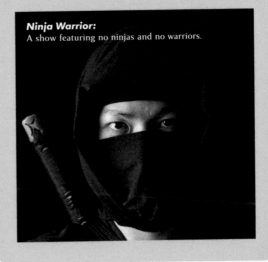

Ninja Warrior:
A show featuring no ninjas and no warriors.

Tom Jnr is now riding that hangover and hitting the 'hysteria' stage.

Tom Malone: It's *Gladiators* for nowadays.

Tom Malone Jnr: It's *Gladiators* mixed with *Total Wipeout*.

Tom Malone: Or *Takeshi's Castle*.

Tom Malone Jnr: I reckon I'd be good at this.

Julie Malone: I reckon [Tom Jnr's elder brother] Lee would be good at this.

Tom Malone Jnr: I reckon I'd be better than Lee.

Julie Malone: No, you wouldn't.

Tom Malone Jnr: Why would Lee be better at this than me? He's stronger than me, but he's not fitter than me. I'm more agile. I can do a flip.

After a few arrogant musclemen fail at the first obstacle and take an early bath, an apparently nerdy 'mobile app developer' takes the podium and starts to make light work of the Quintuple Steps.

Julie Malone: Mr Muscle! Oh, he's thought about it. He's been studying it.

Tom Malone: They're all cheering him along!

Tom Malone Jnr: They never impress me, the nerds, cos they work out the physics of it.

Shaun Malone: He's proper Mr Bean, isn't he?

Tom Malone Jnr: This is the furthest anyone's got.

Tom Malone Jnr
(on Dave the dog):

When Crufts was on, he thought the dogs were behind the TV.

Tom Malone: He's looking at angles and all that, how much velocity he'll need.

Shaun Malone: He's one of them kids that got the Duke of Edinburgh Award.

Much cheering in the living room and in the arena.

Tom Malone: Good jump.

Julie Malone: Swing it, swing it! Jump! Go on, propel yourself! He's like Clark Kent.

Tom Malone Jnr: Not quite: he can't fly.

Mr Muscle falls at the last fence.

Tom Malone Jnr: Knobhead! (to the dog) Get down, Dave, I've got orange juice here. The audience loves an underdog, don't they?

Julie Malone: It was a bit like a Susan Boyle moment.

Tom Malone Jnr: It wasn't.

Tom Malone: This one looks steroid-ed up to the max.

Commercial break. The show is sponsored by Confused.com

Tom Malone: It's sponsored by Brian [the robot from the advert].

Dave leaps up when an advert featuring a dog comes on and stares at the TV as if it's a large picture window, his tail wagging.

Tom Malone: If he sees any animals, he's on it. He watches nature programmes and that. That's what Joe used to do all day.

Tom Malone Jnr: Frank's not that bothered, but he loves beagles. He doesn't care if it's a boy beagle or a girl beagle.

An ad for Pets at Home incites further interest from Dave.

Julie Malone: (to Dave) Ooh look, that's where you have your names engraved, isn't it?

Tom Malone Jnr: When *Crufts* was on, he thought the dogs were behind the TV.

Dave actually barks when a postman comes up the drive.

Julie Malone: We had to get a postbox put up on the outside of the house because postmen were too scared to use the letterbox.

Back at the arena, a dispensing chemist in a bandana takes a tumble.

All: Ohhhhhhhh!

Julie Malone: Makes sure his headband's still in place, though.

Tom Malone Jnr: All these people that think they're fit – they're too muscle-bound for this. You need to be light and agile like a ninja. This woman's got legs like trees.

Shaun Malone: She's gonna fail.

Tom Malone Jnr: Women are always saying they're equal to men, and when it comes to something like this, they're saying, 'We should have an easier course.'

> Shaun Malone:
>
> *He's proper Mr Bean, isn't he?*

Julie Malone: No! Nobody's saying that. You're such a chauvinist. Go on, girl!

An amateur wrestler called Valentine, who thinks he's on WWF, says to camera, 'Ninja Warrior, I will destroy you!' His fate is foretold.

Tom Malone: He's got budgie smugglers on, hasn't he? He's going to struggle on the ropes, being a big lad.

And down he goes.

Tom Malone: Valentine's died a death, there. On the canvas!

Another wrestler steps up. This one's a 'support worker'.

Tom Malone: Support worker? He's got his supports on.

Julie Malone: Hasn't he got funny legs? I hope he goes in. He loves himself too much.

Next is a rugby coach called Cat . . .

Tom Malone: This one's wearing school shorts.

Tom Malone Jnr: Are her shorts on back to front?

Tom Malone: You'd think a Cat would have better balance than that.

Julie Malone: Do you know who I think would be good at this show?

Tom Malone Jnr: Me.

Shaun Malone: Tom thinks he'd be great at everything.

Tom Malone Jnr: I'm basically a ninja already.

The first contestant to actually reach the climactic Warped Wall – a vertical you have to pretty much run up – manages it. He's something in physics. The arena and living room erupt.

Tom Malone: He's a mathlete!

Winning the arena's heart before he's even started is a male model who's also an amputee with one leg, who boldly opts to attempt the course without a prosthetic.

—— " ——

Julie Malone:

Do you know who I think would be good at this show?

Tom Malone Jnr:

Me.

—— " ——

Tom Malone Jnr: He's going to struggle on the mushrooms.

Tom Malone: But he'll have less weight on the ropes.

Julie Malone: They'll have to adapt the course for him, surely.

Tom Malone Jnr: No, because that's discriminating.

Julie Malone: Nobody's gonna laugh at him if he falls.

Tom Malone: To be honest, I might.

He falls off a mushroom. Ben Shephard enthuses, 'He came to prove that he could tackle the course with one leg, and he's done a cracking job.'

Tom Malone: No, he failed miserably.

Julie Malone: He did as good as some of the others with two legs.

Tom Malone: He should have brought the leg with him. I'm not being funny, but he can't be a ninja; you've got to get to the end to be a ninja.

Another contestant claims to be a 'penetration tester'.

Tom Malone Jnr: I don't want to know the ins and outs of that.

Another is a chainsaw sculptor who calls himself a 'country bumpkin'.

Tom Malone: He's got a decent swing on him. It's heightist, this course: the taller you are, the better chance you've got.

The final contestant undermines his timely completion of the course by taking off his vest in victory...

Tom Malone: He's ruined it. Jesus Christ, fella.

Tom Malone Jnr: He looks like he's about to break out into interpretative dance.

Julie Malone: He looks like Screech from *Saved by the Bell*.

Tom Malone Jnr: He went to prison recently.

The heat ends anti-climactically after an hour of pumped-up kicks and Nuremberg levels of adulation with a male-dominated leader board but no winner.

Tom Malone Jnr:

He looks like he's about to break into interpretative dance.

Tom Malone: I'm just happy I witnessed a man called Caradog. Are you just saying it's Welsh because it sounds a bit like 'caravan'?

Julie Malone: No.

When the last 'ninja' has fallen, it's time for me to leave. Tom, a dog's best friend, even gives the family's latest waif and stray (me) a lift back to the station at the end of our session.

Stephen: God definitely happened before him.

Noah

MONDAY, 8.30PM

 In 2015, the BBC broadcast a retelling of the biblical story of Noah's Ark.

 Stephen: Is that Ark?

 Chris: He's called Noah.

 Stephen: I thought he was called Noah Ark.

 Chris: He's not Mr Ark. It's Noah's Ark. It's his ark. 'Noah, you must build an ark …'

 Stephen: I'd be like, 'Bleeding Norah, why did He have to pick on me?'

 Scarlett Moffatt: I'd be like, 'Do I keep the receipts and you can pay me back, or what?'

 Amy Tapper: Why's it called an ark, when it's shaped like that?

 Jonathan Tapper: It should have been called Noah's boat.

 Amy Tapper: An ark is something you walk under.

 Jonathan Tapper: That's an arch, darling.

 Stephen: So was Noah before or after Jesus?

 Chris: I dunno.

 Stephen: God definitely happened before him.

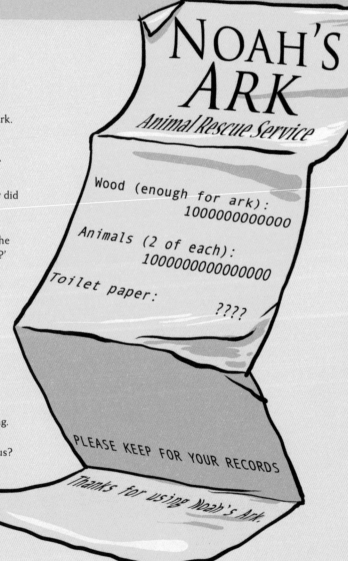

NOAH'S ARK
Animal Rescue Service

Wood (enough for ark): 1000000000000

Animals (2 of each): 1000000000000000

Toilet paper: ????

PLEASE KEEP FOR YOUR RECORDS

Thanks for using Noah's Ark.

GOGGLEBOX
TV

Featuring

THE LETTER 'O'

Including

ONE BORN EVERY MINUTE
OSCAR PISTORIUS
THE OSCARS

EXCLUSIVE! Amy Tapper discusses One Direction!

One Direction

One Direction are a band.
They seem to be quite popular.

Amy Tapper: Aaaaaaaaaaaaaaaaaaaaaaaaaaaaaaaa
aaaaaaaaaaaaaaaaaaaaaaaaaaaaaaaaaaaaaaaaaaaaa
aaaaaaaaaaaaaaaaaaaaaaaaaaaaaaaaaaaaaaaaaaaaa
aaaaaaaaaaaaaaaaaaaaaaaaaaaaaaaaaaaaaaaaaaaaa
aaaaaaaaaaaaaaaaaaaaaaaaaaaaaaaaaaaaaaaaaaaaa
aaaaaaaaaaaaaaaaaaaaaaaaaaaaaaaaaaaaaaaaaaah!

One Born Every Minute

WEDNESDAY, 9PM

CH4 Fly-on-the-wall medical documentary from a hospital labour ward. Not for the squeamish.

Scarlett Moffatt: I take my hat off to these people.

 Scarlett Moffatt: I take my hat off to these people, they're being filmed . . .

 Betty Moffatt: And it's a really private moment.

 Scarlett Moffatt: Because there's a person coming out of your privates.

66

Stephen:

Just think: we're never gonna have that feeling.

Chris:

What, squeezing something out my fanny? Thank God.

99

Oscar Pistorius

South African Paralympic legend and first amputee to win an able-bodied track medal, who was all over the wrong kind of news when found guilty of 'culpable homicide' after shooting dead his girlfriend, thinking she was an intruder in his bathroom.

 Amy Tapper: If he screamed for that person to get out, surely she would just shout out, 'It's only me, calm your tits.'

The Oscars

The most famous motion-picture awards in the world.

 Steph: Wouldn't you love to go to the Oscars?

 Dom: Not really.

 Steph: I would, just to see these exotic animals in their zoo.

 Bill: I think they've improved since they imposed a time limit on the speeches.

 Dom: Gwyneth Paltrow went on for about a week.

 Steph: Her speech at the Oscars will go down as the worst.

 Dom: I'm not entirely sure she's finished. They've wheeled her off, stuck her in a box in the corner.

Oscars Fun Fact

During the Second World War the winners were given Oscar statues made of plaster instead of the usual golden ones, to mark the war effort.

GOGGLEBOX TV

Featuring
THE LETTER 'P'

Including
AGATHA CHRISTIE'S POIROT

Plus
POLDARK POLDARK AND MORE POLDARK

EXCLUSIVE! Watching Poldark with Mary & Giles!

Agatha Christie's Poirot

Classic period detective drama adapted from Agatha Christie's novels, starring David Suchet as the Belgian with the little grey cells. It officially ended in 2013, but left a seventy-episode deluxe box set that will run until the end of the world.

> "
>
> Stephen:
>
> **That's what happens, every time. You wouldn't want him turning up at your party, would you?**
>
> "

Amy Tapper: I'm really confused. Is this a true story?

Stephen: It's always a big country house, a load of people having cocktails – martinis – he rocks up, someone gets mullered and then the whole programme is him trying to find out who's done it. Boring.

Amy Tapper: I like *CSI*, not boring old *Downton Abbey* programmes.

Poldark

SUNDAY, 9PM

BBC1 A 1970s historical tin-mining drama refitted for the twenty-first century with added shirts-off man appeal and HD Cornish views. Aidan Turner became a scything sex symbol as 'Smouldark', the brooding ex-soldier who marries his maid, Demelza.

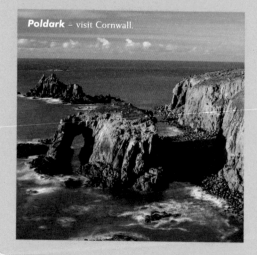

Poldark – visit Cornwall.

June: I love *Poldark*, it's really good.

Leon: Do you like him, June?

June: Ooh, yes.

Jenny: Ooh, he's dishy.

Giles: As far as I'm concerned, this is better than *Downton*.

Stephen: That's like me in my allotment.

Scarlett Moffatt: This is my favourite programme, this.

 Mary: I think he's very good-looking. I'm not sure how good he is at acting, but I'm not sure it really matters.

 Giles: It's Sunday evening. He's setting pulses racing. That's what really matters.

 Tom Malone Jnr: He's always on his horse, looking at the sea.

 Tom Malone: Everything's up and down that one road.

POLDARK TV BINGO

Ross gardening with his shirt off	Some kind of collapse at the mine	Somebody riding on horseback along that Cornish clifftop path that seems to link everywhere with everywhere else
Peasants revealing bad teeth by smiling or snarling	Cameo by the bloke who played Ross in the seventies	George saying something passive-aggressive to Ross and bidding him good day
Putrid throat!	Something about smelting	Demelza getting flour on her nose after baking a tray of cakes

66

Mary:

I think he's very good-looking. I'm not sure how good he is at acting, but I'm not sure it really matters.

99

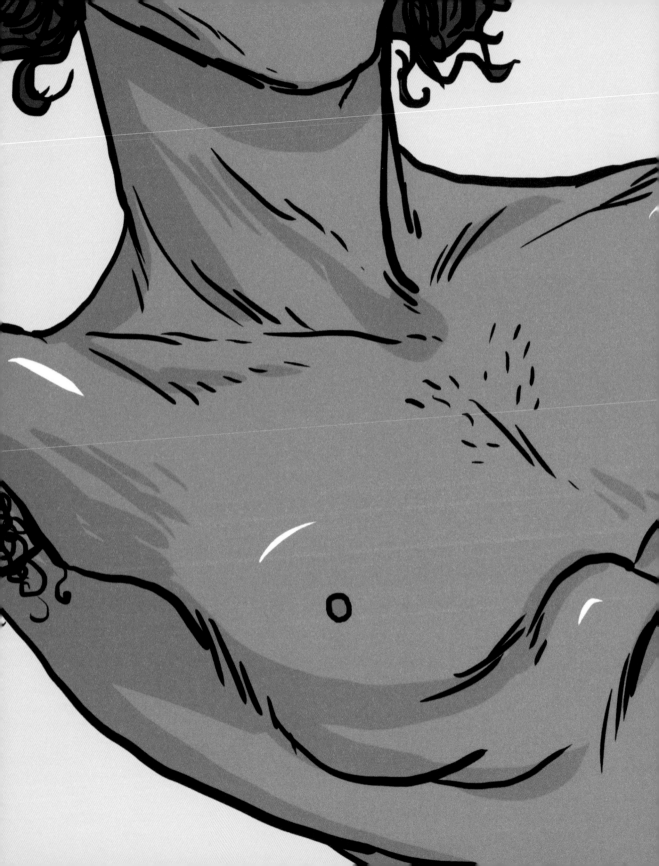

Watching
POLDARK

with MARY AND GILES

When Giles Wood and his wife, Mary, call each other 'Nutty', as they frequently do, it's a term of endearment. Giles says, 'I think it is to do with us both being nuts.' The cab ride from Swindon through undulating Wiltshire countryside to their thatched Hobbit cottage is like going back in time. My driver takes the scenic route – not to fleece me, but to show me the Neolithic stone circles at Avebury.

Giles, an artist who 'enjoys painting the clutter of

> ❝
>
> Giles:
>
> ### *What I love about it, Mary, is the roughness.*
>
> ❞

people's lives', and Mary, a writer, prove uniquely eccentric, disarmingly absent-minded company. Their eldest daughter, also an artist, lives in London; the youngest, a recent graduate, lodges with them. Having knocked on the wrong front door (the cobwebs around the handle should have been my clue that it was unused), Giles emerges further down, as owlish and befuddled as he appears on TV, and leads me, hunched, under low-beamed ceilings, past a downstairs loo being retiled by a local builder called John, to the *Gogglebox* room.

Because my hosts are off on a mini-break to Austria tomorrow, there is washing everywhere. Obscured by a dressing gown hanging from a hook, Mary apologizes for the house being in a 'squalid' state, but it's actually just method bohemian. It smells of old books.

I'm taken by what I believe to be a first edition of *The Golden Bough* by anthropologist Sir James George Frazer (but which turns out to be a second edition) and I like the way a battered CD of Van Morrison's 1972 fusion of folk, R&B and jazz, *Saint Dominic's Preview*, is propped on one bookshelf facing out, as if for sale. Once tea and shortbread are proffered, Giles and Mary gamely clamber into their trademark blanket-draped seats beneath the corner cupboard of legend. The armchair I'm offered groans every time I shift my weight.

They moved here from London in 1988, after Giles sold a 'tiny cottage' in Essex he'd purchased with an inheritance from a great-uncle ('a tycoon in Aberdeen'). Mary apologizes for 'writhing about', but she was thrown to the floor of a London bus on a visit to the Chelsea Flower Show and is 'black and blue'. Giles, who won a piano scholarship to Shrewsbury public school, claims that the alma mater of the chaps who founded *Private Eye* magazine produces 'self-deprecating people, not stuck-up'.

My nutty hosts are anything but. Like any comfortable married couple, they needle and countervail and prompt each other during reminiscences, while Giles plays the deadpan jester to Mary's Celtic queen (he hails from Stoke-on-Trent; she was born and raised in Belfast). A multitasking GP's daughter, she sews as she speaks, possibly darning tights, while wearing bright pink trainers; he, a proud member of the Richard Jefferies Society (a thoughtful Victorian chronicler of rural Wiltshire life), favours unlaced shoes with no socks.

Sitting dead still on my noisy chair for fear of ruining the eighteenth-century cliff-top atmosphere, we gather up to watch the final episode of Poldark, the sumptuous, tunics-off 2015 remake of the 1970s Cornish tin-mine

saga. As Mary actually puts down her sewing to give it her full attention, I start by asking how much of Poldark they have watched.

Mary: Not enough!

Giles: Most of it. But we did miss the last episode, because of *Gogglebox*.

Mary: There are a limited number of things on telly that are pleasant to watch and not alarming.

Giles: What I love about it, Mary, is the roughness. The trouble with living in Wiltshire is it's very manicured, isn't it?

Mary: Yes.

Giles: I like seeing the wild flowers and things, rough landscape. Someone said the tin miners weren't dirty enough. Their hair was too clean.

The two horny-handed servants, played by Phil Davis and Beatie Edney, exchange pearls of unaffected wisdom in broad Cornish accents, wearing rags.

Mary: That's a bit like me.

Giles: That's a bit like me as well. The trouble is, we are a bit like the servant couple. If I took my glasses off… Yeah, he's definitely like me.

Mary: See the way he's eating without teeth in? That's a good authentic touch. I looked up *Poldark* on Wikipedia and apparently it is many, many, many books that he wrote. Winston Graham was born in something like 1910 and he is one of the first people to be named after Winston Churchill.

Giles: The interiors are very beautiful. This one looks like a Vermeer.

Mary: They must have exclusively hired women, actresses, who did not need make-up.

The main attraction is Aidan Turner, who plays Ross Poldark. I ask, 'Do you empathize with the armies of women – and, I'm sure, men – who fancy him?'

Mary: Yes, he is lovely looking.

Giles: Ooh, this is the beginning of the putrid throat.

Mary: Look at that little boy. God, we are so spoiled today compared to them with all the things they could get: TB, putrid throat, polio, cholera.

Giles: Well, they didn't have antibiotics. I'd have been dead the next day.

Mary: My cousin died of polio.

Giles: Was it her, Demelza, who has caused this problem?

Yes. Poldark risked scandal by marrying his own kitchen maid, the flame-haired Demelza, who idealistically brokers the elopement of his sister with a disgraced sea captain, which leads to some argy-bargy about Ross's smelting operation.

Giles: Demelza thought they were entitled to happiness.

Mary: How do you think they filmed that long shot? Helicopter? Because the horse would be spooked otherwise…

Maybe they used a drone. Did you watch this in the 1970s?

Giles: Only vaguely. But it wasn't something we would always watch.

Mary: But in the seventies, Nutty, we were clubbing and stuff. We weren't watching telly.

Giles: Sunday nights segued nicely from *Downton* into this. For a nation that is supposed to be getting rid of the class system we are obsessed with the class system, really. From our love of *Upstairs, Downstairs* to *Downton* we actually quite admire societies where everybody knew their place.

Mary: You do, love.

Giles: Well, no, I don't, because the person I identify most with is Gordon Jackson from *Upstairs, Downstairs*; neither upstairs nor downstairs. He knows his place. I feel ill at ease in drawing rooms. I'd like to be the Lord of Downstairs.

Mary: Everything about *Poldark* is so lovely…the costumes…

Giles: The compositions all look like paintings. George Romney or an interior Chardin or something. High production values.

We listen to a dastardly speech from Poldark's banking nemesis George Warleggan, one of a new breed of industrialist, played by Jack Farthing.

Giles: He's a baddie.

*He was in the film **The Riot Club**.*

Giles: Was that the one about the Bullingdon? Did you know that, Mary? He was in *The Riot Club*. Poldark was sold down the river by his cousin who got drunk. I can't remember quite the mechanics of it. But he's lost everything now. You see, unlike *Wolf Hall*, although it's lit by candles, you can still see, whereas in *Wolf Hall* you couldn't see anything. Demelza is getting better at bossing people around now.

> **Giles:**
>
> ## Sunday nights segued nicely from **Downton** into this. For a nation that is supposed to be getting rid of the class system we are obsessed with the class system, really.

Mary: Is that Brian Blessed?

No.

Giles: This is like Thomas Hardy: it just piles misery upon misery, almost so that you can't bear it.

George is still lording it over Poldark, who's lost control of his mines.

Giles: You just want to thump him, don't you? As a villain, he would be the equivalent now of a 'bankster'. You know, Morgan Grenfell. Don't you think, Mary, they are the new villains, the banksters?

Mary refuses to rise to Giles's bait.

Giles: We don't always sing from the same songsheet, do we, Mary? Unlike some couples we know. Mary's always been a staunch Tory. But I've gone anti-globalization. Occupy. Green. The scales have fallen. Conservatives don't know how to conserve any more.

Mary: I'm not entirely Tory. It's *faute de mieux* [for want of something better].

Giles: Look how beautiful that is! That is a Claude or a Turner. Absolutely beautiful. Some of these tin mines were shot at a place in Cornwall called Botallack, because I have been there. Look at those uniforms.

Mary: God, he is gorgeous. Look at him.

Giles: You see, I think that we are recovering now from that dreadful period when Tony Blair tried to banish history, like Pol Pot or Ceauşescu. He tried to pretend we didn't have a history we could be proud of. He hated history and thought it was irrelevant.

Cool Britannia?

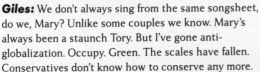

Mary:

Everything about Poldark is so lovely... the costumes...

Giles: And the Dome.

Mary: What I would like to know is, what money was generated in the local area of Cornwall as a direct result of this? It's very good for modern Britons to see what life was like in those days.

Giles: I bet sales of candles will go up after this. Do you remember Price's Candles in Battersea?

That factory has closed. But the company still trades.

❝

Mary:

What I would like to know is, what money was generated in the local area of Cornwall as a direct result of this?

❞

Mary: Candles may soon be outlawed on health and safety.

Giles: I'm very keen on English candles…beeswax.

A few hours with Giles and Mary is a tonic. Though they only have a dusty Digibox on top of the TV (and had no TV for the twelve years up to 1999), they are no Luddites. When my Dictaphone packs up, Mary's iPhone records the last twenty-three minutes and she kindly offers to transcribe the conversation for me, which she has done by the time I get back to London that night. There's a lot of ancient energy around the regally messy, artistically inclined Giles and Mary, but no wi-fi signal.

GOGGLEBOX TV

Q

Featuring
THE LETTER 'Q'

Including
QI

Plus
THE QUEEN

And
QUEEN B

QI

WEDNESDAY, 10PM

BBC2 The show for dead-brainy people. And the rest of us.

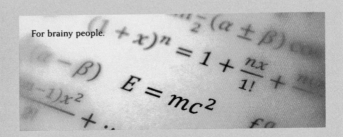

For brainy people.

The Queen

Her Majesty the Queen Elizabeth II has reigned for more than six decades.

Steph: I love the Queen.

Sandra: That lady's the best woman in the whole wide world.

Sandy: Do you think she farts? I do; quiet ones. *Peep*.

Umar Siddiqui: What does she do?

Sid Siddiqui: Well, you can't sum it up in one sentence, all the things she does. There are lots of things you wouldn't even begin to understand about what she does.

Umar Siddiqui: You don't know, do you?

Sid Siddiqui: Well, no, not in detail.

Sandra: I have a dream that I will meet the Queen and she will acknowledge me.

Leon: The Queen gets on my nerves with her sour face and so on. She's waited on for everything; they probably dress her like they do in *Downton Abbey*. They probably even put her knickers on. If she wears them.

June: Oh God.

Umar Siddiqui: Who gives the Queen her telegram when she gets to be a hundred?

Sid Siddiqui: Well, Charles will hopefully be King by then.

Baasit Siddiqui: Hopefully? That's treason.

Chris: I could tweet her 'from one old queen to another'.

Stephen: You'll get beheaded.

"

Sandra:

*That lady's the best woman
in the whole wide world.*

"

GOGGLEBOX TV

Featuring
THE LETTER 'R'

Including
ROME
THE ROYALS
RUSSELL BRAND

EXCLUSIVE! Carolyne Michaels is starting a revolution!

Rome

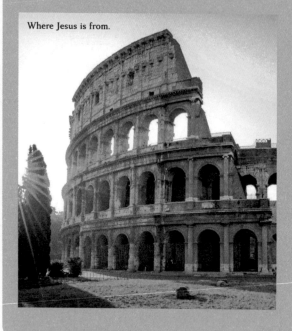

Where Jesus is from.

Sandy: Is that where Jesus is from?

Sandra: Lots of stuff. Rome, Rome, Rome. The Greeks. Cleopatra and all that.

——— 66 ———

Leon:

**Country of love, Juny.
I make-a-love-a to you later.**

June:

In-a your dreams.

——— 99 ———

The Royals

SUNDAY, 10PM

 In this new show broadcast on E! the Queen is played by Liz Hurley.

Umar Siddiqui: Is this treason?

Russell Brand

Dandyish comic firebrand and swordsman who told his one million Twitter followers not to vote, then to vote Labour. Whenever he appears on TV, the Goggleboxers have varying reactions.

 Leon: I believe he's quite a womanizer, Russell Brand.

 Andrew Michael: He's a monster, look at him.

 Chris: He's clean now and he's given up drinking.

 Stephen: He don't do anything now apart from yoga.

 Steph: God, he needs a slap.

 Louis Michael: He's a real person, who's experienced the real world.

 Andrew Michael: He's clearly immoral.

 Chris: I'm listening to him but it's going over my head.

 Stephen: Is there anything you'd like me to help you with?

 Chris: No. Because you're thick too.

 Carolyne Michael: Who doesn't realize he's a genius? There is going to be a revolution and we'll be behind you.

 Sid Siddiqui: So, anyone who's not with you is against you. And you shoot them.

 Baasit Siddiqui: Yeah, it's quite dangerous what he's saying, isn't it?

 Dom: I don't think he'll find me voting for him, purely and simply because he seems to still be on acid.

 Steph: And he looks dirty.

GOGGLEBOX TV

S

Featuring
THE LETTER 'S'

Including
SCENES OF A SEXUAL NATURE
SCHOOLDAYS
SCOTLAND
SPIDERS

Plus
STRICTLY COME DANCING
STEPHEN HAWKING
STAR WARS: EPISODE IV
SUSAN BOYLE

EXCLUSIVE! Steph & Dom's GUIDE TO SEX!

Scenes of a Sexual Nature

Sandy: A man's G-spot is in his bottom.

 Bill: The first European to write about the clitoris was a man called Columbus in 1516.

 Amy Tapper: If Mum had, like, A-cup boobs, would you still have married her?

 Jonathan Tapper: Probably not.

 Nikki Tapper: I can't actually believe you just said that.

 Jonathan Tapper: What I'm trying to say is that I might not, with the first impression. You came up to me, but it might not have got any further, but it obviously did because of your personality. And your big tits.

 Sandy: A man's G-spot is in his bottom.

 Sandra: Shut up!

 Sandy: Go find out.

 Sandra: I don't want to know.

 Leon: I'm sure, even today, some women aren't having orgasms. If their husbands aren't experts.

 Bill: The first couple shown in bed together on prime-time TV in the USA were Fred and Wilma Flintstone.

 Stephen: My friend was going through her loft and she found an old magazine with a photo of Phillip Schofield sunbathing in a pair of Speedos, so she took a photo of it and tweeted him and he replied, saying, 'Oh my God.'

 Chris: God, really?

 Stephen: Looked like he had a big todger on him.

 Scarlett Moffatt: Your ears line up with your nipples. Your nipples and ears are for balance.

Scarlett Moffatt:

Your ears line up with your nipples. Your nipples and ears are for balance.

 June: (can't help smiling)

 Leon: Ha ha!

 Carolyne Michael: [Andrew] drags me into an Ann Summers every time we walk past one.

 Alex Michael: (to her dad) You are a dirty old man.

 Sandy: Some womans' pum pums is like a tunnel – big!

 Leon: Do you find me more attractive now I'm slimmer?

June: I'd find you more attractive if you talked a bit less.

 Sandy: So young girls not getting pregnant, because all the mens are having sex with virtual-reality girls on the computer.

 Viv Woerdenweber: There's a photograph of you with a bra on.

 Ralf Woerdenweber: *Ja.* After twenty pints.

 Leon: You did a strip once on that cruise ship.

 June: What?!

 Leon: We were encouraging you.

 June: That was line dancing.

 Alex Michael: (to her mum) That's so weird, you're the only one out of all of us without any Greek in you.

 Carolyne Michael: Well, I have had some Greek in me.

ON NUDISM

 Leon: I walk naked round this house. Not downstairs, upstairs.

 Chris: I don't have a problem being naked. When I have my spray tan, I'm naked.

 Stephen: What, in front of the woman?

 Chris: Yeah.

 Stephen: You don't put the pants on?

 Chris: No.

 Stephen: You let her see your willy?

 Chris: Yeah.

 Tom Malone Jnr: Everyone loves getting out the shower and swinging free for a bit, but you wouldn't want to live like it.

> 66
>
> Tom Malone Jnr:
>
> ## *Everyone loves getting out the shower and swinging free for a bit, but you wouldn't want to live like it.*
>
> 99

 Tom Malone: I'd miss walking around with my hands in my pockets too much.

The Goggleboxers were fascinated to learn that many mammals have a baculum or penile bone.

  Leon: So if I had a penis bone, I'd be able to have sex a hundred times a day?

 June: If you got out your armchair.

 Leon: I'd miss the telly.

 Stephen: A hundred times a day? I can just about manage once a week.

ON POLYGAMY

 Baasit Siddiqui: So he spends three nights with one wife, and three nights with the other. What does he do with the spare night?

 Sid Siddiqui: He rests.

Umar Siddiqui: He just sits there with his balls in a big bucket of ice.

Schooldays

 Stephen: I hated school. I used to spend the time looking out the window.

 Rev. Kate: I was short, fat, round, spotty, ginger and a Christian. Bullies had a field day with me.

 Scarlett Moffatt: School was traumatic for me. I had teeth that could eat an apple through a friggin' letterbox. And a monobrow.

Scotland

In 2014, Scotland voted to stay as part of the United Kingdom.

Ralf Woerdenweber: I didn't understand a word they were talking about.

 June: I'm glad they're staying in the United Kingdom.

 Ralf Woerdenweber: I didn't understand a word they were talking about.

 Josef: Why the Union happened in the first place: Scotland was bankrupt and England said, 'We will bail you out if you join us.' So my answer now is, 'Yes. You want to go separate? Fine. But can we have our £400 billion back please?'

Spiders

Documentaries about the creepiest of creepy-crawlies bring out the arachnophobes of Gogglebox.

Dom: Nasty, hairy, shiny, fat-arsed, jizz-covered-handed monsters.

 Dom: All those legs and arms, how does she know which one's his knob?

 Ralf Woerdenweber: So the female spider has sex with the male and then the female eats the male. I would be gay.

 Stephen: If I was a spider, I'd be like, 'Alright, love, have you had lunch, fancy a shag? I promise you we'll go and get something to eat after.'

 Dom: Nasty, hairy, shiny, fat-arsed, jizz-covered-handed monsters.

 Steph: You've just described the best part of the House of Commons, haven't you?

Chris:

I hate spiders. Some of them have really big Kim Kardashian arses, don't they?

Star Wars: Episode IV – A New Hope (1977)

 Currently six-, soon-to-be-seven-part space saga which began long ago, in a galaxy far, far away…from inventing CGI.

 Nikki Tapper: It's such a load of shite.

 Stephen: It looks shockingly cheap.

 Josh Tapper: Where's *Star Wars* set?

 Jonathan Tapper: In space. It's called *Star Wars*.

 Leon: June…come to the dark side and show me your knicks!

 Stephen: He's been on the Benson & Hedges, this one.

 Leon: I'd be delighted if Darth Vader was my father. Big strong fella.

 June: He could look after you with your big mouth.

 Leon: The only thing is, how did he ever make love to anyone with that big uniform on?

JUNE… COME TO THE DARK SIDE AND SHOW US YER KNICKS!

STEH AND DOM'S

GUIDE TO SEX

Steph, 49, and Dom, 51, have been married for seventeen years. They live in Kent with their children Max and Honor, and Squidge the sausage dog. Their upscale guest house gave the well-lubricated pair their first taste of TV on the reality show *Four in a Bed*, in which B&B owners swap establishments. Dom also appeared on Channel 4's winter-themed celeb sport-off *The Jump*, but was eliminated in the second round. They also played host to a certain party leader with a well-exercised pint-raising elbow in *Steph and Dom Meet Nigel Farage*. Although keen observers of all things televisual through the bottom of a tumbler or champagne flute, their minds are apt to wander to matters carnal. Enlightenment for those of us at home always ensues.

"

Dom:

Sex is like air, really. It's only important when you're not getting any.

"

Steph: I can remember watching TV with my parents and this sex scene [coming on] and I can remember my mother always saying, 'Oh dear, she's obviously not feeling too well, they're taking off her shirt so she can cool down.'

Dom: Really?

Steph: Yes.

Dom: I've never watched porn with my parents.

Dom: Sex is like air, really. It's only important when you're not getting any.

Steph: Women look from bottom to top.

Dom: I thought that was men who did that.

Steph: No, men do boobs, right down. Women do crotch and up. That's how it works.

Dom: I must be a woman.

Steph: You are: a lesbian trapped in a man's body.

Dom: Why do people having sex on TV always keep their bras on? It's one thing if you're having a quickie, but if you're having a longie, surely you take the whole lot off?

Dom: What do you want [to drink] now?

Steph: It depends if you want to have sex, really.

Dom: What does that mean?

Steph: If you want to have sex, I'll have vodka Red Bull. If you don't, I'll have something gentle that'll put me to sleep. So surprise me.

Dom: Well, that's not going to be tricky, is it?

Steph: Please God, let it be a Baileys.

Steph: (drinks tequila)

Dom: You look like you've stuck your tongue up a baboon's arse.

Steph: What's a buttery nipple [cocktail]?

Dom: Sounds disgusting.

Steph: Slippery nipple.

Dom: What's in it?

Steph: Sambuca and Baileys.

Dom: Sounds like filth.

Steph: It makes me start singing and taking my clothes off…

Dom: OK, where's the sambuca?

Steph: I wonder, could you tell [which were my tits in] a line-up, blindfolded? Could you tell my tits by feel?

Dom: Blindfolded? No, I don't think I could.

Steph: You disappoint me. I reckon I'd know your knob. I reckon I would.

Dom: In America, they haven't seen a pube since 1983.

Dom: Last night, I dreamt I saw Jennifer Aniston's bush.

Steph: Why the f**k are you having dreams like that? You shouldn't tell me things like that.

Dom: Well, is there anything you'd like to tell me about?

Steph: No. I have nightmares, and you're dreaming about Jennifer Aniston's nether regions.

Dom: Well, I didn't ask for it.

Dom: There's a place called Fannyhands Lane, Butthole Road, Nob Fields, Fanny Street, Bummers Hill. Which is just above Nobland Green.

> Dom:
>
> ### Last night, I dreamt I saw Jennifer Aniston's bush.

Stephen Hawking

Theoretical physicist, cosmologist, author and Director of Research at the Centre for Theoretical Cosmology at the University of Cambridge, he was also the first person to set forth a unifying theory of cosmology making use of the general theory of relativity and quantum mechanics.

Baasit Siddiqui: He's from England, isn't he? But his voice sounds American. Do you think he's got it on the wrong setting?

Chris: When he was younger, he looked like Deirdre Barlow.

Strictly Come Dancing

SATURDAY, 6.30PM

BBC1 Eleven-year-old celebrity ballroom-dancing competition presented by Claudia Winkleman and Tess Daly, previously presented by Sir Bruce Forsyth until he was encouraged into belated retirement.

Leon: You're a good dancer, aren't you, June?

STRICTLY COME DANCING TV BINGO

Anton partnered with the more mature female celebrity	Kristina partnered with the young, male hunk	Someone who can't dance doing slightly better at the jive
Visible weight loss	Public votes someone useless back in	Public keeps voting someone useless back in, again and again
Craig saying 'daaaaahling'	Bruno saying something ever so slightly over the top	Len saying 'sev-ahhhhhhhhn'

Rev. Kate: The good thing about having Tess and Claudia and not Brucie is that I'm not frightened someone will die live on television.

 Tom Malone: I could do this here.

 Julie Malone: Could you?

 Tom Malone: I've got the figure for it.

 Ralf Woerdenweber: I'm not drunk enough to watch.

 Dom: You used to boogie. You used to stack the shelves. You taught me how to drive the bus.

 Steph: Sixteen years you've been telling me this, and it's bullshit.

 Dom: It's not bullshit. You just can't remember. You were so smashed.

 Leon: You're a good dancer, aren't you, June? I have to hold on to you, though, in case my legs give way.

 Scarlett Moffatt: Sir Bruce Forsyth is just four months older than sliced bread.

Susan Boyle

Defied all kneejerk sexist, ageist, fascist expectations on Britain's Got Talent in 2009 by not singing like she looked, then took over the world, performing for the Queen and never changing.

 Stephen: Her hair could be a lot better. I mean, there's not a lot you can do about the face.

 Sandra: She'll get an OBE. The Queen loves her. That's a virgin and a woman of substance. Like me. But I'm not a virgin.

GOGGLEBOX TV

Featuring
THE LETTER 'T'

Including
TAKEN
and
TITANIC
in our Movie Review special!

Plus
24 HOURS IN THE PAST

Taken

Liam Neeson stars as a father out to rescue his kidnapped daughter, using his 'very particular set of skills'.

———— 66 ————

Scarlett Moffatt:

I'd be shaking like a shitting dog. What would you say, Dad? 'I have a set of skills. Fabricating welding skills. I have a sat nav. I will find you.'

———— 99 ————

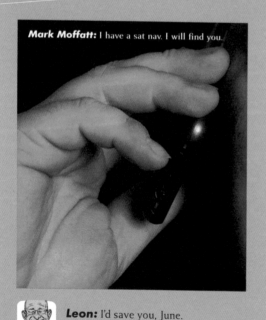

Mark Moffatt: I have a sat nav. I will find you.

Leon: I'd save you, June.

Titanic

Spoiler alert: it sinks.

Amy: Was the Titanic real?

Leon: It was a tragedy that should have been avoided. But the love story in this is brilliant.

Tom Malone Jnr: She's a bitch: there's enough room on that bit of wood for both of them. There's loads of ways they could have got on it together; all she had to do was sit up. Then she pushed him into the water at the end.

Amy Tapper: Was the *Titanic* real?

"

Stephen (watching Kate and Leo embrace on the prow of the boat):

I wonder how many people have gone to the front of the Calais ferry and done that?

"

Watching
24 HOURS IN THE PAST

with REV. KATE AND GRAHAM

Fully expecting to take a local cab from the station, I am flummoxed to see the unmistakable, compact but collarless figure of Rev. Kate at the other end of the platform. She runs melodramatically in mock slow motion towards me. The only thing missing is steam, although later on this morning, she'll provide masses of smoke, as we shall see. The twenty-minute shuttle in a hatchback full of the evidence of parenthood allows the talkative, Yorkshire-born clergywoman, 40, to offer a guided tour of the rural Nottinghamshire district that contains her three – yes, three – churches. I confess I can't take it all in.

> **Rev. Kate:**
>
> *They're only doing this because* **I'm a Celebrity** *didn't phone them.*

Kate has come to regard *Gogglebox* as her 'fourth parish', and welcomes strangers coming up to talk to her. 'It's kind of what I'm in the gig of being a vicar for.' If she and violin-teacher husband Graham, 47, have an agenda, it's 'Look, we're Christians, but we're not complete dickheads!' The Irreverent Reverend challenges many more preconceptions, admitting to a 'girl-crush' on Siobhan the PR in *W1A*, and describing High Anglicanism as 'bells and smells'.

The downstairs loo is a gaudy shrine to gift-shop religious ephemera and novelties that dare you to question their piety: 'nearer thy God to pee'.

I can't help but be reminded of the comedy *Rev*, even though it's set in the inner city and we're in a village whose website lists only two local businesses. The vicarage here, too, is an open house. I'll flatter myself that the feast on the dining-room table, which is warping under the weight of cold meats, bread, dips, salad, organic ale and homemade, Nigella-recipe 'Guinness cake', has been laid on just for me, but if the local poor turn up unannounced, I think they'll get my chair.

Graham gets back from walking Buster the greyhound. He attributes the non-appearance of their two children, Ruby and Arthur, to 'the age of Zoella and iPads and headphones and incommunicado for teenage offspring'. Although it's Ruby who shouts down the breaking news that Kate's namesake, the Duchess of Cambridge, has had a baby. The Rev.'s reflex action in an internet age is to put on the telly to confirm the tidings, with perhaps a little more fervour than you'd expect from a republican.

When the pre-lunch coffee and Waitrose 'Seriously Gingery' dark chocolate biscuits come out, I'm honoured to get the 3D Jesus mug and approve of the equally denominational knitted Yoda tea cosy, plucked from the overflowing hamper of cosies. I'm also excited to spot what I believe to be the very milk jug that Buster was once caught drinking from – a religious relic of sorts, if it's not sacrilegious to say so.

We tuck into the lunch, but not before Kate starts sniffing the air and remembers she's left a loaf of bread in the oven. A burnt offering, it has calcified to a black brick and she sensibly chucks it out onto the back lawn, swinging wide all downstairs windows to release the acrid smoke before it sets off the fire alarm. Bells and smells, indeed.

Willingly squashed between the Rev. and Graham – and with Buster snoozing to our left, tackle safely stowed downwards – we take up our mugs, scoff another Waitrose Seriously Gingery and settle in for 24 Hours in the Past.

24 Hours in the Past

TUESDAY, 9PM

 A 'living history' fig leaf gives academic weight to this four-part dressing-up stunt in which six celebrities – ranging from former Tory Home Office minister Anne Widdecombe to *Outnumbered* teen heart-throb Tyger Drew-Honey – work for food and shelter in a number of grim Victorian scenarios, some involving a shovel and what comes out of a horse.

Rev. Kate: Oh, that's Tyger Honey-Whatsit. I do often wonder how many more celebrity formats there are – how many more things can we get celebrities to do? Obviously what they've done when they've pitched this is gone, 'This is very worthy cos it's all about history and it's to get young people into history,' but actually it's just a thinly veiled excuse to make celebrities look stupid and shovel shit. Oh, please lock up the Tory MP in the jail! I hope Alistair McGowan is gonna do loads of impressions while he's doing it. I feel sorry for impressionists. Everywhere they go, it's: 'Do that, do that!' Anne, it's time for a breast reduction and time to have your hair cut. That was terribly against the sisterhood of me, but I don't like Anne Widdecombe. She left the Church of England because of women priests. Sometimes, as a woman, you feel obliged to like all women. The exception is Katie Hopkins…What's made them want to do this?

Graham: To be on telly?

Rev. Kate: They're only doing this because *I'm a Celebrity* didn't phone them.

Colin Jackson says he is excited about being able to 'literally go back in time'.

Rev. Kate: (whoops with genuine pleasure) *Literally* go back in time! Yes! I love it when people use the word 'literally' incorrectly! A parishioner once said to me, 'It's been a brilliant year because I've literally been set on fire by God.' Ha ha ha – aargh! Can you imagine some poor little runner having to go and fetch that horseshit? Wait a minute: has Anne Widdecombe rested her breasts on her suitcase?

We rewind to confirm. Yes, she appears to have positioned herself in repose while leaning on the extended handle of her wheelie suitcase. Much merriment.

Rev. Kate: Hooray! That's worth a BAFTA alone!

Graham: It's 2D, you can't see the depth.

Rev. Kate: This is brill. I love humiliating celebrities. I forget that they're real people. Mind you, they're getting paid for it, so...

Graham: Are they actually living there or at the end of the day does a car pick them up and take them back to the hotel?

Rev. Kate: Oh, it's *her*.

Historian Ruth Goodman.

Rev. Kate: She's on everything. It reminds me of that Channel 5 reality show where the woman who'd allegedly had an affair with David Beckham tossed off a pig. (noticing a blonde actress) Who's that actress? I'll have seen her playing a cadaver in *Holby City*.

It's Zöe Lucker.

Graham: This programme is dire.

Rev. Kate: Is that Mel Giedroyc doing the voiceover? I just had the taste for cake.

On the drive back to the station, I feel full of chorizo and ale and the lamb of God, and have a friend; if not in Jesus, certainly in Kate. She apologizes, then apologizes for apologizing, for being so interested in the royal baby. 'It's like liking white bread,' she parables. 'You know you really shouldn't, but you can't help it.'

Amen to that.

Through the power of TV, we take you back to 2011

UK Riots, 2011

The summer 2011 reboot of early 1980s riots, also sparked by inflammatory London policing and racial tension, but snowballed via BlackBerry to include Birmingham, Bristol and Manchester. Flatscreen TVs and trainers were liberated from local businesses, thus sticking it to 'the man', rather than 'The Man'. We watched a news report from the second night and everyone had a different experience of those events.

Rev. Kate: I was really proud of Sheffield during the riots. They didn't riot. Steel City not Steal City.

 Graham: It was the only region that didn't riot.

 Rev. Kate: It's completely understandable. It was Charles Dickens's 'best of times, worst of times', because it brought out the worst in people and the best in people.

 Jenny: Oh, that was awful. Can you imagine what it was like for all them people in the war? The worry of that coming to you.

 Lee: It was all them shops, wasn't it? They just wanted to loot, didn't they? It was all over nothing.

 Scarlett Moffatt: I forgot this happened.

 Betty Moffatt: They have these riots and they get that big you forget the reason why the whole thing started. 'Sorry, why are we looting?'

 Scarlett Moffatt: It makes no sense. It's like shitting on your own doorstep. It's like us going down the Metrocentre and smashing windows up and going into the town and throwing paint – no one else would suffer but us. The rioting didn't get up here.

 Mark Moffatt: It got to Manchester.

 Betty Moffatt: We haven't got that much stuff to smash up.

Rev Kate:

I was really proud of Sheffield during the riots. They didn't riot. Steel City not Steal City.

 Scarlett Moffatt: You go to some parts and it looks like they've already rioted.

 Tom Malone Jnr: I was stuck in the middle of it in the centre of Manchester. I went to dance training and Dad had to come and get me. I walked out and that side of the road (gestures) were people in balaclavas and all sorts, and that (gestures to the opposite side) was a line of police in riot gear. Someone was smashing the window of Tesco's with a bike. I thought, you're going to ruin that bike.

 Nikki Tapper: We were away. We were in Israel. And I was petrified. I didn't want to come home. I remember my friend sending me a message saying, 'Don't come home.' It finished the day we came home.

 June: I'd forgotten about this. Our daughter lived in Ealing. You don't think about this sort of thing happening in Britain. Normally people are quite calm about things.

 Louis Michael: This is exactly what's happening in America now.

 Stephen: This is the reason I moved to Brighton. Me and me mum were living above a row of shops on the Roman Road Market in Bow, and they all robbed them and I just thought, I don't wanna live amongst these people any more. So me and me old mum came down here. I knew all the kids that were looting the shops, and everyone was leaning out of the windows, and they weren't telling them to stop, they were going, 'What you got? What you got to sell?' Me and my brothers and sisters were right little bastards, but I asked them all, 'Do you think we'd have got roped into all that?' And they were like, 'No way.' There were people who'd never nicked a penny chew in all their lives who went in and nicked a bottle of water, and then got done for it. They didn't know why they'd done it.

Sandra: Riots are for free TVs. I don't agree with them.

Sandy: You're not helping anybody, you're just destroying the place. The other day, in Brixton, why did they mash up windows in a charity shop and a Foxtons? It's pathetic.

An anti-gentrification demonstration had turned nasty and damage was done to an estate agent's.

Sandy: It's sad. They do it for all the wrong reasons. It's like football violence. They set it up and go down there. The thing with the riots this time is that it was black, white, Indian, Chinese … it was everybody. All of the youth want their jackets, their trainers, their flatscreen TVs, everybody wants it.

Sandra: And what about Black Friday?

Sandy: That's another bad thing that come from America! We don't need those things here. It's like they want to change England into America. I don't get it. Food banks? It's going back to the old times. It's Victorian. What is happening right now? The rich are getting richer and the poor are getting poorer.

Eve Woerdenweber: I was in Blackpool with my nan, and even though the riots weren't up there, I remember you telling me that the riots had been in Birkenhead, and I was shitting myself. I was like, 'I don't wanna come home!' There was a shop in Prenton got burned down, a hairdresser's.

Ralf Woerdenweber: They covered all the windows up in Birkenhead Shopping Centre. And shop owners stayed at their shops overnight.

———————— 66 ————————

Stephen:

This is the reason I moved to Brighton. Me and me mum were living above a row of shops on the Roman Road Market in Bow, and they all robbed them and I just thought, I don't wanna live amongst these people any more. So me and me old mum came down here. I knew all the kids that were looting the shops, and everyone was leaning out of the windows, and they weren't telling them to stop, they were going, 'What you got? What you got to sell?'

———————— 99 ————————

University Challenge

MONDAY, 8PM

BBC2 Hardest quiz on telly, in which plain students from one uni battle identical ones from another uni. 'Getting one right' is an air-punching moment for most viewers.

Scarlett Moffatt: They need to go out and get drunk, instead of reading books all day...

 June: You like this, don't you?

 Leon: I do. I don't answer many questions. But I like watching these bright young men and women.

 Betty Moffatt: Anyone who gets a question right on this gets excited.

 Sid Siddiqui: Why do they have to make the questions so hard?

 June: I think these students are geeks.

 Leon: They're not like we were, bonking every night.

 Baasit Siddiqui: Not one of these guys has been touched by the sun, have they?

 Scarlett Moffatt: (pretending to introduce herself on the show) My name's blah-de-blah. I'm reading classics, yah? And I have never kissed a girl.

 Jenny: (doing the same) Hi, I'm Jenny Newby. I'm reading the *OK!* magazine.

 Betty Moffatt: They all look like people that are really old.

 Scarlett Moffatt: They need to have a good night out. Go out, get drunk, instead of reading books and shit all day. (on realizing there is no prize for the triumphant team) Do they not even win dictionaries?

 Jenny: (assessing the contestants) I tell you, I'd marry *him*. He'll have a good job when he's older. He'll always be at work.

 Tom Malone Jnr: I got three questions right on *University Challenge* last time.

 Julie Malone: I got two.

 Tom Malone Jnr: I got a question right that the people from Cambridge and Oxford didn't get right. I can't remember the question but the answer was carbon.

 Julie Malone: They were pretty clever on the final.

 Tom Malone Jnr: Not as clever as me, apparently.

 June: You're not just a pretty face.

 Leon: Shut up.

GOGGLEBOX TV

Featuring

THE LETTER 'V'

Including

VIRTUALLY FAMOUS VIRAL VIDEOS

Plus

THE VOICE

EXCLUSIVE! Watching Virtually Famous with the Moffatts!

Watching
VIRTUALLY FAMOUS
with THE MOFFATTS

 Carrying the accumulated scent of the five Woerdenweber cats and essence of Malone Rottweiler, I arrive at the Moffatt family's tidy terrace in County Durham as an olfactory time bomb for a shih-tzu. First, formal introductions with the uprights: the softly spoken Mark, 49, who opens the door, the family's dark horse Betty, 45, and zinger-ologist Scarlett, 24, perched, as she does, on the sofa. While Custard Creams are passed round, we establish for the record that Scarlett's nine-year-old sister is Ava Grace Moffatt, named after Ava Gardner and Grace Kelly.

Scarlett Sigourney Moffatt is named after O'Hara and Weaver.

> 66
>
> Scarlett Moffatt:
>
> ## Gogglebox *is like the theatre; Big Brother's *panto.*
>
> 99

'You liked Scarlett and I liked Sigourney,' Mark reminds his wife. 'So we had a game of Scrabble to decide.' She won. 'It was a close game, though,' he adds. Scarlett sums up, with characteristically theatrical indignation, 'So I'm named after a whore and someone who gives birth to an alien?' Betty jumps in: 'I wouldn't say Scarlett O'Hara was a whore.' No, she was keeping it all together during a very turbulent and difficult time. Mark adds, 'She did what she had to do to stay afloat.' It's typical of a night in with the tangential and enquiring Moffatts that we've already referenced two films and a novel, and the TV has yet to get involved.

Scarlett wears her approval ratings lightly, batting away media curiosity and shrugging off overtures with touching brand loyalty ('*Gogglebox* is like the theatre; *Big Brother*'s panto'). And when her dad boasts that she's followed by Harry Styles's sister on Twitter, she's entirely circumspect: 'Yeah, she's got nearly two million followers. And that's just his sister!' I'm not the first to recognize the unadulterated adoration with which she's regarded by her parents onscreen, even if she's blissfully unaware. 'You are funny,' Mark tells her. 'I'm not,' she bats back. Scarlett admits she's actually grown closer to her mum and dad since the show. 'We go for food together and that now.'

At this point, the shih-tzu, Harry, named after Prince William's brother, is allowed in after some scratching – and reacts to my cocktail of pet smells accordingly by throwing himself at me and barking like crazy.

Harry is still licking my face, and the remaining four humans pass round the biscuit barrel as we watch Virtually Famous.

Virtually Famous

MONDAY, 10PM

E4 A closing-time comedy panel game show on E4, essentially based around YouTube clips of weird people, viral phenomena and dogs falling off things. It is hosted by Kevin McHale, best known for pretending to be in a wheelchair on *Glee*, and its team captains are hairy comic Seann Walsh and blameless Scott Mills-sidekick Chris Stark. It goes quiet for a moment as the show begins …

Scarlett Moffatt: He's the one in the wheelchair on *Glee*. (turns her attention to the people on the panel) He's off *Made in Chelsea*. He's on *The Last Leg*. She's off *Snog Marry Avoid* – she's been on something else, but I can't remember what. It's weird to see that guy out of his wheelchair – he's got legs.

They are fascinated by the odd face colour of guest Dappy.

Mark Moffatt: What's Dappy got wrong with his face? Why's it all tight?

Betty Moffatt: He's got fake tan. He's had some sort of facial.

Scarlett Moffatt: Oh, they're showing the photo where he's got his massive tail out. It only looks massive cos he's little.

Has it been doctored?

Scarlett Moffatt: No, that's just his third leg.

Betty Moffatt: It doesn't look like a real beard – it looks like it's been drawn on.

Mark Moffatt: Is Dappy wearing that tan so we can't tell he's blushing?

The man from Made in Chelsea appears to be a living self-parody and actually uses the word 'yah' for 'yes'.

Scarlett Moffatt: 'Yah'! He's even got posh teeth, hasn't he?

Asked to guess why two 'special guests' are internet-famous, the panel are shown three choices, the first of which is 'drone boners': basically gay sex filmed from above by a drone.

Mark Moffatt: I've never heard of drone boners before.

Scarlett Moffatt: Dad, it isn't a thing. It's not a trend.

Mark Moffatt: Oh, right.

Scarlett Moffatt: They do look dirty.

Another choice is a clip of One Direction performing 'Story of My Life' but 'shredded', which means a bad vocal is laid over the top of Harry Styles's beautiful one.

Mark Moffatt: That is classic.

Betty Moffatt: I would think they'd look really embarrassed but they don't.

The special guests reveal that they are the 1D 'shredders' and have 'received a few misspelled death threats'.

Scarlett Moffatt: One Direction only have to put 'I'm going in the bath' and they get like a million retweets. It's ridiculous! It is actually mental. Me and our Ava watch way too many YouTube clips. We watch *X Factor* fails all the time. Hours of it.

A woman in the next clip lifts a full pint glass using her teeth and downs the pint.

Betty Moffatt: Oh my God!

Mark Moffatt: That is amazing. Wow.

The panellists attempt to copy the stunt, including the posh man, who says, 'I don't know where to start.'

Betty Moffatt: Usually, with the glass.

Mark Moffatt: I can't see him doing it, though.

Scarlett Moffatt: Do you think he's ever drunk a pint before? I can't drink pints, mind. I don't think I could even pick up an empty glass with my teeth.

Mark Moffatt: Have you ever tried a yard of ale? With a bowl on the end? I have, a few times.

Scarlett Moffatt: He's drowning in beer.

Betty Moffatt: It's gone up his nose.

Now, a 'what-happens-next?' round called 'Nail or Fail?', where a clip is paused before its outcome. An American approaches a ramp over some washing machines in a mobility scooter.

> "
>
> Scarlett Moffatt:
>
> ## One Direction only have to put 'I'm going in the bath' and they get like a million retweets.
>
> "

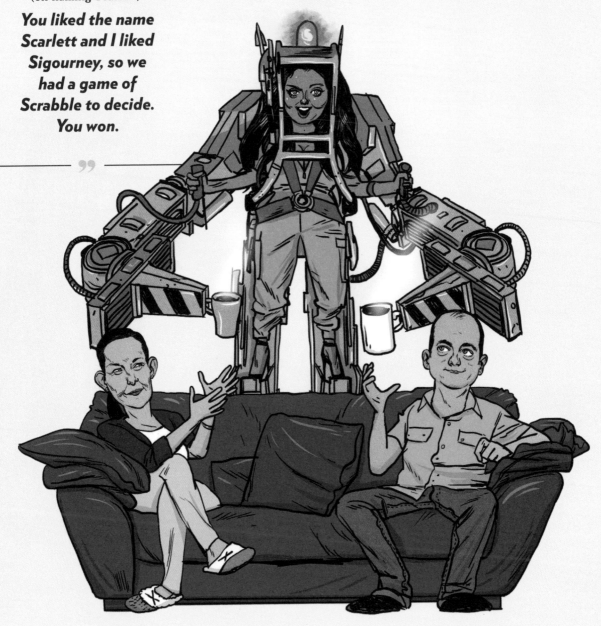

> **Mark Moffatt
> (on naming Scarlett):**
>
> *You liked the name Scarlett and I liked Sigourney, so we had a game of Scrabble to decide. You won.*

> ❝
> Scarlett Moffatt:
>
> *I might film you
> dancing, Dad, and
> put it on YouTube.*
> ❞

Scarlett Moffatt: I think he's gonna nail it, cos he looks that stupid.

Mark Moffatt: The first board's gonna flop down, look.

Betty Moffatt: He's got to fail.

He nails it.

Scarlett Moffatt: Only in America.

Next, a 'double slo-mo dog dive', in which a pooch attempts to reach a sofa.

Scarlett Moffatt: He's gone way too early. It is funny seeing a dog fall over sometimes. See? Fails are always better in slo-mo. I might film you dancing, Dad, and put it on YouTube. This is alright, this, actually.

Team captain Chris is challenged to sit still and smile while panellists and guests attempt to distract him. First, a man with a python.

Mark Moffatt: That wouldn't bother me.

Scarlett Moffatt: It wouldn't bother me.

Next, some gunge.

Scarlett Moffatt: Oh, it's like being back in the kids' TV days, with the gunge.

Next, a sweary old non-league football fan called 'The Wealdstone Raider', who went viral in late 2014 before almost having a Christmas number one.

Scarlett Moffatt: Oh, I love this, this went massive! Have you never seen this? It's a classic! It's only, like, thirty seconds long but it went everywhere.

Then a male stripper comes on. The show seems to have fallen apart.

Mark Moffatt: Eurgh!

Betty Moffatt: Eurgh!

Scarlett Moffatt: What is this? What is this show? It's gone from being funny to being friggin' ridiculous.

Mark Moffatt: Does anyone want a brew?

Scarlett Moffatt: Put lots of milk in mine.

Betty Moffatt: She never drinks it.

Gently extracting Harry from my face, I leave the lively Moffatt home with Scarlett playfully baiting her mum about fancying Gregg Wallace.

Scarlett Moffatt:
You fancy Gregg Wallace, don't you?'

Betty Moffatt:
I do not fancy him. At all.

Scarlett Moffatt:
You always talk about him.

The Voice

SATURDAY, 7PM

BBC1 Meritocratic karaoke contest in which the twist is that the panel judges don't know what the singer looks like, for about a minute.

Umar Siddiqui: This has always been *X Factor*'s nicer cousin, hasn't it?

As a contestant sings 'Careless Whisper'...

Scarlett Moffatt: Oh my God, George Michael will be turning in his bloody grave.

Betty Moffatt: He's not dead.

Scarlett Moffatt: I get him mixed up with Elton John all the time.

Betty Moffatt: He's not dead either.

Scarlett Moffatt: Well, he hasn't brought a song out for a long time.

THE VOICE TV BINGO

Will.i.a.m saying a performance was 'dope'	Tom Jones mentioning that he sang with Elvis	Judge going to press button, then pulling their hand away
Contestant spinning a sob story out of a normal scenario ('I stubbed my toe')	Judges whispering about whether they're going to push the button or not	A singer saying that this is their last chance
A judge starting to dance to get some attention	Someone putting their feet up on the ledge of the button	Ricky's expression revealing that he has experienced the sudden, deathly realization that he used to be quite cool

GOGGLEBOX TV

Featuring
THE LETTER 'W'

Including
WALRUS
THE WEATHER
WEEKEND ESCAPES WITH WARWICK DAVIS
WHO SHOT J.R.?

Plus
WOLF HALL

Walrus

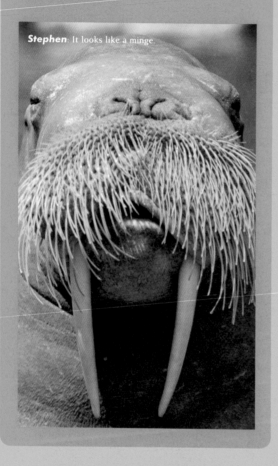

Stephen: It looks like a minge.

Stephen: It looks like a minge.

Steph: What was that Beatles song about?

Dom: If you're in a dance club and you think you're an eggman, you're off your tits on something.

Steph: Very true.

The Weather

There's nothing the English love more than talking about the weather. The Goggleboxers are no exception.

Ralf Woerdenweber: Germany is trained because every year we have snow. So nothing stops.

 Sandy: It's all twisted. When it's meant to be summer it's winter, when it's winter it's summer, when it's spring it's autumn. The whole world's going off its head.

 Sid Siddiqui: It's global warming, isn't it?

 Baasit Siddiqui: You can't just say that about everything without the facts.

 Sid Siddiqui: I have better facts than your fact it's not.

 Baasit Siddiqui: Go on then.

 Sid Siddiqui: Well…

 Baasit Siddiqui: That's a good fact.

> 66
>
> Sandy:
>
> *It's all twisted. When it's meant to be summer it's winter, when it's winter it's summer, when it's spring it's autumn. The whole world's going off its head.*
>
> 99

Watching
WEEKEND ESCAPES WITH WARWICK DAVIS
with THE WOERDENWEBERS

To enter the house of the Woerdenwebers is to enter a house of magic. I even travelled here via a glowing, serpentine underground portal: the Birkenhead Tunnel. Whether you believe that cats are witches' familiars or not, there are five living here, mostly glimpsed in groups of two or three. Like the Malones' dogs, you sense that the humans feel privileged to lodge with Shadow, Sybella, Mr Tabby, Imbri and Bliss. Bliss, a rescue, sleeps soundly, curled on a red cushion on the industrial black corner sofa with us all evening, but it is the playful, vocal Shadow with whom I become the most familiar.

> ❝
> ## *Viv and Eve used to belong to the English Civil War Society.*
> ❞

Earlier, on this dark, stormy night in the fabled Wirral, my talkative taxi driver dropped me off just as Eve, 21, Ralf, 52, and Viv, 53, were trooping, in single file, up to their front door, all home from work and college at the same allotted time. This sight speaks of their co-operative unity and we soon warm up in their cosy living room with coffee, chocolate biscuits and ginger cake amid the candles and sacred pebbles. (Oreo ice creams are distributed later.) A bookcase is crammed with George R. R. Martin, Stephenie Meyer, Philippa Gregory and a couple of Paul McKennas.

Dragons, Egyptian pharaohs and Hollywood stars adorn the walls (there's Clark Gable kissing Vivien Leigh's cheek), and what *Gogglebox*'s only German, Ralf, bluntly introduces as a 'new cupboard' is, in fact, a full-height glass display cabinet filled with crystal, goblets, candlesticks, curios, feline figurines and a palmistry hand – what I imagine Viv's New Age shop in Birkenhead Market to be like.

If she's amethyst, Ralf's rock – a rock drummer, in fact (he plays an electronic kit at home and makes the 'hanging round with musicians' joke before I can). Music is a uniting force; the couple first met at a gig and have recently been to see Adam and the Ants. Viv wears the T-shirt – black, of course.

For further psychological profiling, Ralf's mug says 'Let There Be Rock', Eve's says '21', and Viv's says 'Wonderful Wife'. (He's a big man, but Ralf is a teddy bear.) Viv and Eve used to belong to the English Civil War Society. They were in the Cavalry and Viv once cooked curry in a cauldron.

Droll drama student Eve is eager to share a *Harry Potter* 'fan theory' with her equally *Potter*-partisan mum: 'Have you ever wondered why the Dursleys were so horrible to Harry?' If, like Viv, you think it's because Petunia hated her sister because she wanted to be a witch and wasn't, you're so wrong. 'No,' Eve continues with glee, before losing me completely. 'Remember how the Horcrux made Ron? Harry was a Horcrux: try living with a Horcrux for ten years. It would make them horrible.' Food for thought in a house like this.

'J. K. Rowling,' Eve reports gravely, 'has yet to confirm.'

Mortified to have to rouse Bliss from her red cushion so that I can occupy the corner position of their death-metal-black couch, I note that

she quickly curls up elsewhere as we help ourselves to one last piece of ginger cake. We sit down to watch this affable travel show.

Weekend Escapes with Warwick Davis

FRIDAY, 8PM

ITV *Harry Potter* star Davis traverses these isles looking for leisure with his equally compact wife and two kids. Never has his size been such a non-issue. We are viewing the second episode of the second series, a merry jaunt through South Wales. The pre-episode montage reveals a treat in store for historical re-enactor Viv …

Viv Woerdenweber: Oh, there's some historical re-enactment!

Ralf Woerdenweber: What you don't understand is how difficult it is for these tiny people to do things that we don't even think about.

Viv Woerdenweber: The world is for tall people, isn't it? I can't reach the top shelves in the supermarket.

The Davis clan are to join some 'living history' enthusiasts and are pre-dressed as Vikings. Warwick says, 'I just hope we don't have to stop for petrol!'

Viv Woerdenweber: We've stopped at service stations in full dress and it's been very funny. I didn't catch where they're going. Oh, it's in Wales.

They make camp in the grounds of St David's Bishop's Palace, which dates back to the sixth century.

Viv Woerdenweber: He's got his authentic Viking dog.

Warwick leaves his wife and daughter 'grinding corn' while he and his son go and do some 'pillaging'.

Viv Woerdenweber: I'd rather be firing a bow and arrows!

Ralf Woerdenweber: He's saying a woman belongs in the kitchen.

Eve Woerdenweber: The helmet's too heavy for his head!

Viv Woerdenweber: Viking women actually did go on the field and fight.

'Have you done amateur dramatics, Viv, because historic re-enactments are essentially acting?' I ask.

Viv Woerdenweber: No, but you've got to be a drama queen to do it. We're drama queens, aren't we, Eve? You have to get into the role. Especially if you're gonna fight a battle, because we used to field about a thousand people in the English Civil War Society.

Ralf Woerdenweber: If I do one step, Warwick Davis has to do three or four.

Viv Woerdenweber:

We've stopped at service stations in full dress and it's been very funny.

Viv Woerdenweber: (giggles) He's going to go and pillage a shop! But he has to watch out for the CCTV, something the Vikings didn't have to worry about! He's below the CCTV.

Ralf Woerdenweber: In reality, in two minutes the police would be there.

Viv Woerdenweber: In Viking times, there was no police.

Eve Woerdenweber: What's he doing?

Warwick is pillaging some boiled sweets from the driver of a car who's stopped at some lights. Next, father and son try a bit of 'bushcraft' in the woods, camouflaging themselves, lying in the grass and hoping their dog won't find them. It does actually walk past them. Now to make fire.

Viv Woerdenweber: They'll probably burn the forest down.

Ralf Woerdenweber: You're not allowed to make fire in the forest.

Some I'm a Celebrity-style grub-eating goes badly.

Ralf Woerdenweber: Where's he going?

Viv Woerdenweber: He's going to spit it out.

He's in Harry Potter, which you love.

Viv Woerdenweber: He's Griphook, and Professor …

Eve Woerdenweber: Flitwick.

Next stop: Llanwrtyd Wells for the World Alternative Games, featuring worm charming …

Ralf Woerdenweber: He's found a worm and now nobody will touch it and put it in the bucket.

… and bog snorkelling. Warwick is somewhat handicapped by his size and the fact that he can't swim.

Viv Woerdenweber: I can't swim and I wouldn't go in.

Ralf Woerdenweber: When I was growing up, I can't think of anyone who couldn't swim.

Viv Woerdenweber: We're an island and lots of people can't swim.

> 66
>
> Ralf Woerdenweber:
>
> ## He can take the piss out of himself, and not a lot of people can do that.
>
> 99

Ralf Woerdenweber: Get in the water, mate! Of course it's cold, it's not a bus. And they didn't warm the water up for you.

Viv Woerdenweber: He's going backwards! This is family entertainment.

Ralf Woerdenweber: I think it's a brilliant programme, I really do. He can take the piss out of himself, and not a lot of people can do that. What I really love is that he shows his kids: be normal and have fun. And that for a parent is good. You may not be the tallest in the world, but have fun, enjoy your life, be yourself.

When it's time for me to leave I feel as if I've just experienced the best advert for the European union. It transpires that Viv understands more German than she speaks, but this is a household where innate, unspoken understanding casts a spell. Viv was impressed when Ralf first took her to his homeland and challenged her to find a single speck of dust in the hotel's breakfast room. She couldn't ('It was so clean'). Before I go, the Woerdenwebers literally herd cats, cooing them in from outside to meet me. It is with some regret that I eventually have to disappear.

Who shot J.R.?

The 'Who killed Lucy Beale?' of the three-channel 1970s, when oil-rich US soap *Dallas* had lead baddie J. R. (played by Larry Hagman) shot at the end of the 1979–80 season – the highest-rated TV episode in US history – leaving the world wondering for eight long months. We sit down and watch one of the most famous moments from a soap opera ever.

 Rev. Kate: You wouldn't have seen this, Graham, because you didn't have a telly. It was Kirsten that did it. It's a great pub-quiz question. Our family weren't big *Dallas* fans but even we watched this. We were more of a *Knots Landing* family. Do you know what the ranch is called, Graham?

 Graham: Southfork.

 Rev. Kate: Well done, your education is going well. It doesn't look that posh now, does it?

 Jenny: Who shot J. R.? That was a big thing.

 Lee: I used to watch it, until bloody Patrick Duffy came back. He went into that shower. F**king long shower he had. Was it Sue Ellen who killed J. R.?

 Jenny: It was Bing Crosby's daughter!

 Lee: What was she called?

 Jenny: Shut up a minute while I'm thinking, I'm going through the alphabet. Crosby?

 Lee: Crystal?

 Jenny: Kristin!

 Betty Moffatt: I used to love *Dallas* when I was a kid. Do you know who shot him?

 Scarlett Moffatt: It was a woman, wasn't it?

 Betty Moffatt: Yeah, it was a woman. I think we thought it was Sue Ellen but it was her sister, Kristin.

 Scarlett Moffatt: And why did they shoot him?

 Betty Moffatt: He was just a dirty rat.

 Mark Moffatt: He was a rotter.

 Scarlett Moffatt: Was it a bit like 'Who shot Phil Mitchell?'

 Mark Moffatt: I used to sit in and watch *Falcon Crest* with me mam before I went out.

 Betty Moffatt: As a kid when I watched it, I always thought it was really glamorous. It was a bit like how the other half lived. You didn't eat al fresco in the eighties; it wasn't done. Even when they went to bed they looked beautiful, with big hair. I watched *Dynasty* and *The Colbys*.

 Mark Moffatt: I used to like *Man from Atlantis*. That was classy. Webbed hands.

 Giles: Wasn't there someone called the Poison Dwarf?

Mary: I watched it occasionally and I did like it. I remember someone I worked with saying to me, 'I had no idea how the rich lived before, and now I've seen it, I want it for myself.' I think it did have that effect.

 Julie Malone: I never used to watch it. I think I was at Morris-dancing practice at the time.

 Nikki Tapper: This was one of the best programmes ever. I remember this clearer than the Berlin Wall.

 Josh Tapper: Why was it a big deal if he didn't die?

 Amy Tapper: Was it like 'Who killed Lucy?'

 Jonathan Tapper: Much bigger than that.

 Nikki Tapper: It was Pamela, wasn't it?

 Jonathan Tapper: No, it was Cliff.

 June: Sunday night, everybody used to rush to sit down to this. It was in the papers. I can't remember who did it. Not his wife?

 Leon: He recovered, didn't he?

 June: He used to curl his lip.

 Leon: Bobby was hopeless.

 June: He was just a pretty boy, wasn't he?

 Chris: I never watched this. I liked *Dynasty*. Big shoulder pads.

Stephen: When we watched this we had a 50p slot on our TV, and we'd always sit there thinking, just f**king go off before the end. That's how skint we were.

 Andrew Michael: We loved *Dallas*!

 Alex Michael: I don't even know what it is.

 Andrew Michael: When I was in my early twenties and decided to go into business, I modelled myself on J. R.

 Carolyne Michael: It was on the front pages of all the newspapers! It looks laughable now – there's no blood, there's no gore!

 Louis Michael: That's the worst shooting scene I've ever seen.

 Andrew Michael: My beloved mother used to make me a cup of coffee at ten past eight on a Wednesday night and I would go in and watch *Dallas* with her.

 Sid Siddiqui: That was the daddy of the soaps. There was nothing else to compare.

 Baasit Siddiqui: I didn't know you watched this, Dad. You were a right little soapy.

 Umar Siddiqui: Lee Harvey Oswald, wasn't it?

> Andrew Michael:
> ## *We loved* Dallas!

 Ralf Woerdenweber: J. R., you hated him but you loved him at the same time. He was a hate–love character.

 Viv Woerdenweber: This was like 'Who killed Lucy Beale?'

 Ralf Woerdenweber: And after this came *Falcon Crest*.

231

Wolf Hall

WEDNESDAY, 9PM

BBC2 Slow-burning six-episode digest of Hilary Mantel's historical novels, with theatre's Mark Rylance as cunning advisor Thomas Cromwell to Damian Lewis's not-that-fat Henry VIII. An intense, authentic evocation of life in Tudor England, it was heralded by critics and viewers alike.

 Baasit Siddiqui: Apparently they spent a huge amount of money on candles. The candle budget is ridiculous.

 Scarlett Moffatt: I know it's like as if it's actually the olden days, but for the purposes of actually being able to see, what the f**k is going on? Can someone please turn a light on?

 Baasit Siddiqui: God, no one would be able to see us at all. We'd have to be smiling constantly.

 June: It's obviously done deliberately, but you can't see anything.

 Chris: Why not just light more candles?

 Stephen: And have some more characters. Why not go on a nice horse ride?

Tom Malone: In the olden days, they didn't used to look at each other much, did they? Look: he's talking, she's looking out the window.

Umar Siddiqui: (quoting the show) 'Does not Mistress Seymour have the tiniest hands?' That's cos you're looking at her from far away.

The programme's authenticity included the use of the C-word at one point.

 Scarlett Moffatt: Absolute lad. He just dropped the C-bomb in a period drama.

 June: Ooh, getting a bit naughty now.

 Sandy: That's wicked, that's dirty.

 Mary: Mark Rylance: the facial repertoire was a bit limited.

 Giles: The bourgeoisie was shocked by some of the more fruity language.

 Mary: Is there still a bourgeoisie, do you think?

 Giles: Oh yes.

IS NOT MY MISTRESS FAIR?

GOGGLEBOX TV

Featuring
THE LETTER 'X'

Including
THE X FACTOR

The X Factor

SATURDAY, 6.30PM

ITV By overwhelming consensus 'not as good' as the similarly Simon Cowell-dictated star factory *Britain's Got Talent*, this is the talent show that makes aerobic karaoke singers worse by making them better. And gets them the Christmas number one.

The X Factor: Not as good as *Britain's Got Talent.*

> ❝
>
> Stephen:
>
> *I wonder if after every series Simon Cowell changes his phone number so none of them can get hold of him any more.*
>
> ❞

 Josh Tapper: Amy thought the X in 'X Factor' stood for xylophone.

 Stephen: I'd just look up and say, 'Shit.' I wouldn't even say 'that was'. Then I'd look down.

 Andrew Michael: I've said it before but it's like a Victorian freak show.

 Jonathan Tapper: It's so predictable.

 Stephen: I wonder if after every series Simon Cowell changes his phone number so none of them can get hold of him any more.

 Scarlett Moffatt: I like songs where you can air-grab. Push it out, pull it back in.

 Julie Malone: I'd love to go see [special guest] the Bublé.

 Tom Malone: Oh, he's a bag of shite.

 Sandy: Why does everybody always cry?

 Sandra: I'm crying.

 Sandy: Let me get you a tissue.

 Sandra: I've got one but it's got curry on it.

 Sandy: That's why you're crying.

 Chris: I love Dermot. Tight trousers.

 Stephen: Dirty bastard.

On the final…

 Baasit Siddiqui: You get nervous, don't you?

In 2013, it was tenser than ever…

 Amy Tapper: I'm scared I'm gonna do a poo.

Sandy:

Why does everybody always cry?

Sandra:

I'm crying.

Sandy:

Let me get you a tissue.

Sandra:

I've got one but it's got curry on it.

Sandy:

That's why you're crying.

THE X FACTOR TV BINGO

You, realizing that you're already impatient for the return of *Britain's Got Talent*	Louis quitting/ rejoining/both	The ghost of Dermot O'Leary glimpsed during the opening number
Simon stopping a song midway through and demanding a contestant starts again	The current series making minor adjustments to minimum/maximum age and categories	Someone who sings like Ed Sheeran
Someone who sings like Ellie Goulding	Female judge perving over young, male contestant in act of post-feminist empowerment	Simon Cowell wins

GOGGLEBOX
TV
Featuring
THE LETTER
'Y'
Including
YOLO
EXCLUSIVE! You do only live once!

YOLO

In February 2015, in a piece about President Obama filming a viral video on the US healthcare system, the BBC felt the need to explain that YOLO stood for 'You Only Live Once'.

Stephen: Bit like saying 'hashtag something'. Not really very street.

June: Did you know it meant that?

Leon: Yeah. Not as good as N.O.R.W.I.C.H. though – 'Knickers Off, Ready When I Come Home'.

Stephen: It's a bit late in the day for that one, isn't it? Bit like saying 'hashtag something'. Not really very street.

Chris: Is 'YOLO' the new 'hashtag'?

Stephen: F**k knows.

Tom Malone Jnr: He's quoting Drake there, 'YOLO'.

Tom Malone: Sir Francis Drake?

Tom Malone Jnr: (stares)

Tom Malone Jnr:

He's quoting Drake there, 'YOLO'.

Tom Malone:

Sir Francis Drake?

Tom Malone Jnr:

(stares)

GOGGLEBOX TV

Featuring
THE LETTER 'Z'

Including
Z CARS

Z Cars

> Leon:
>
> *You need something beginning with 'Z' to end the book with? We used to watch Z Cars.*

Acknowledgements

Like the tortoise who'd been mugged by two snails said to the police: 'It all happened so fast.' One minute I was a *Gogglebox* viewer – or, professionally, a reviewer – the next I was on the other side of the glass, watching telly with its beloved stars in their own homes and drinking from their mugs.

To visit all the households on my favourite factual entertainment programme of the twenty-first century, in person, took a lot of logistical know-how and military planning. For making it happen, I have a number of people to thank. *Gogglebox* executive producer Tania Alexander, cast manager Harriet Manby and production manager Gemma Scholes at Studio Lambert made all the introductions and smoothed my passage into some of the most famous living rooms in Britain, arming me with just the right amount of foreknowledge. Jamie Coleman at Pan Macmillan was editor, foreman and travel agent, adept at all three, with Zennor Compton on hand when he wasn't. Steve, Abi and the north London crew never once made me feel in the way. For encouragement, Jason Hazeley, one of only two outsiders to have made that epic journey before me; and for illustrative genius, Quinton Winter. Thanks to solicitors Haldane, Wylie & Legge for an impromptu night out at Ye Cracke in Liverpool. Back in the real world, my *Gogglebox*-loving family were an appreciative first audience for my traveller's tales, and Julie cheered me on through some late shifts at home.

I'd like to thank my manager Rob Aslett and Bella Lamplough Shields at Avalon for moving the furniture around me. And a doff of the cap to all those lovely people at Channel 4, especially David Glover.

But a special thank you to those who welcomed me into their homes and made me feel less like a travelling sales rep and more like an old friend. In the order that I met them: Josh, Jonathan, Amy and Nikki; Kate, Graham, Ruby and Buster (Arthur was out); June and Leon; Jenny, Lee and Ray; Bill and Josef; Eve, Ralf, Viv, Bliss, Shadow, Mr Tabby, Syb and Imbri; Tom, Julie, Tom Jnr, Shaun, Izzy, Lucy, Dave, Frank and Bob; Mark, Betty, Scarlett, Ava and Harry; Baasit, Umar and Sid; Chris, Stephen, Ginge and Fred; Sandy and Sandra; Giles and Mary; Louis, Alex, Carolyne and Andy. All back to ours!

Andrew Collins,
London, June 2015